KU-483-099

Contents

Fundamental Aspects of Research for Nurses

Sue Dyson and Peter Norrie

QUAY
BOOKS

A division of MA Healthcare Ltd

Quay Books Division, MA Healthcare Ltd, St Jude's Church, Dulwich Road, London
SE24 0PB

British Library Cataloguing-in-Publication Data
A catalogue record is available for this book

© MA Healthcare Limited 2010

ISBN-10: 1 85642 378 6
ISBN-13: 978 1 85642 378 6

Printed by CLE, Huntingdon, Cambridgeshire

Preface

The Prime Minister's Commission on The Future of Nursing and Midwifery in England published its final report on 2 March 2010. Front Line Care states that nurses and midwives must renew their pledge to society to deliver high-quality compassionate care, thus placing quality of care at the top of the healthcare agenda. Responsibility for this must lie with nurses, midwives and their employers. Central to this is the requirement for nurses and midwives to understand and undertake research, development and evaluation as a prerequisite for thinking innovatively to influence system design in health care and positively impact on service delivery. In short, nurses need to be at the forefront of strategic leadership and decision making in healthcare, and this requires a thorough grounding in research, commencing with pre-registration training and continuing throughout a professional career. This book provides the initial grounding in research and recognises the importance of introducing research to nurses in a straightforward and understandable format. It is an introductory text and positions the student nurse as an autonomous learner with a responsibility to enhance their understanding by following up references and through further reading. Suggestions are given for appropriate sources to supplement each chapter.

The book is designed to introduce the student to the world of research and takes a conventional approach, considering qualitative and quantitative research separately. We begin in Chapter 1 with an overview of research philosophies and paradigms. We consider the centrality of the research question and the literature review in determining the research design. We introduce quantitative and qualitative research methodologies. Chapter 2 provides an overview of qualitative research methods, focusing on ethnography, phenomenology, grounded theory, action research, feminist research and narrative methods. Chapter 3 discusses methods for collecting qualitative data, including sampling strategies and methods for data analysis. Chapter 4 concludes the section on qualitative research, considering issues of quality and ethics. Chapters 5 and 6 are concerned with quantitative research, including an exploration of the two most popular types: the classic scientific experiment and the use of surveys to explore populations. Quantitative data analysis is discussed in Chapter 7, which includes some exercises for those who are wary of statistics. In Chapter 8 we include a discussion of mixed methods in research, acknowledging the shift away from strict adherence to one particular approach to one which places the research question centrally in determining the most appropriate research design. Finally, we conclude with a discussion of evidenced-based care and the significance of this for nurses and nursing practice.

Acknowledgements

Sue Dyson would like to thank Simon Dyson for his constant encouragement, not only in writing this book but in all her endeavours. Thanks also to Emma and Matthew McCartney for being a constant source of joy and to Rehana Dyson for giving her the pleasure of being a step mum.

Thank you to all the pre- and post-registration nursing students who have provided a forum for her research teaching over the years, without too much complaint.

Most of all thanks to my dad who has been and always will be my greatest fan. This book is dedicated to him.

Peter would like to thank his wife, the inestimable Mrs Norrie (known to her friends as Sarah), and his marvellous children, John and Catherine, for their humour and support. Thanks also to my brother Alan; given that this may be my only book, I thought it would be best to include him.

Thanks also to my father Tom; gone but still around.

CHAPTER 1

Ways of thinking about research

Introduction

In this chapter, we discuss the philosophical basis of research. By this we mean the extent to which researchers believe on the one hand that we are active in creating or shaping the social world in which we live, or on the other hand that the social world exists independently of what we may think of it. On first reading this paragraph you might already feel lost, thinking that research is too deep, detailed, complicated and not for you. This is understandable if you are new to research and has much to do with unfamiliar terminology for what are actually quite straightforward ways of thinking about important questions and how best to find the answers . While research may be detailed, can be complex, and may involve groups of people with very different views about a particular issue, it is nevertheless something you can undertake. Indeed, you would not be reading this book if that were not the case. Therefore the most important point to make, at the outset, is that you can come to understand the philosophical basis of research, and begin to understand how your own worldview shapes the kinds of research you may want to undertake.

It is important to note that the approach advocated in this chapter is not without its critics. Authors have pointed out that holding fast to a philosophical position at the outset can inhibit our understanding, as it precludes the possibility of an alternative viewpoint (Dyson and Brown, 2006). For example, if we were to ask student nurses for their views on why attrition rates from nursing courses are high we are approaching the research question from the philosophical position that it is possible to understand the social world in which the student nurse lives. The alternative position is that it is not possible to understand how the student nurse perceives the world with any degree of certainty; therefore, we need other forms of knowledge to answer the question of why attrition rates from nursing courses are high. Our method of enquiry, should we view the world this way, might be to collect information (data) about numbers of students with higher entry qualifications, types of qualifications, age, gender, and ethnicity and to look for relationships with patterns of attrition (Dyson *et al.*, 2008).

In spite of criticisms of an approach where the researcher has a predetermined idea of how we can come to know the world, an advantage is that the researcher can more readily apply a structured and logical approach to designing and carrying out the research. Certainly, for beginning researchers this is a most useful approach. However, it is important (and indeed the position taken in this book) that the beginning researcher strives to keep an open mind. Dyson and Brown sum up this position when suggesting that researchers who adopt a philosophical viewpoint at the outset may use it as a cloak against other philosophical positions. While this approach has the attraction of consistency it may lead the researcher to believe they have found the one '*true*' philosophical position to the exclusion of all others (Dyson and Brown, 2006, p. 3).

Research philosophies

What do we mean by philosophies of research or ways of knowing the world? If we take a standard definition of philosophy as being a belief or system of beliefs accepted by an individual or group of individuals we could begin to understand that it is possible for individuals or groups to hold different beliefs about the same thing. More to the point, individuals or groups might consider their views authoritative, with or without evidence to support the particular belief. For example, an individual may hold the view that 'sparing the rod spoils the child', whereas a group or organisation such as the National Society for the Prevention of Cruelty to Children (NSPCC) might take a different approach and hold the view that smacking any child, for any reason, is inherently wrong. When placed in the context of research, philosophy is about how we can come to know the social world in order to understand why practitioners and users of health and social care services think and subsequently act in the way they do. For example, we may ask the question why, in spite of evidence to the contrary, do individuals continue to engage in unhealthy practices such as smoking, excessive drinking, and overeating. Similarly, why do a significant number of health and social care practitioners engage in similar practices when we could argue that the first group may be excused, as they know no better, while the second group should know better through their exposure to specific health education. Of course, this is to oversimplify what is occurring, as we know there are many factors influencing individual health behaviour. For researchers in health and social care, interested in exploring these phenomena, or manifestations of behaviour, we need to know something about research philosophy if we are to understand the fundamental problems for practitioners and users of health and social care services and to ask the right questions in the right ways.

It is generally accepted that there are two main, although not exclusive, ways of coming to know the social world, by which we mean the world inhabited by social beings or communities as opposed to the world of the individual or biological entity. These distinct philosophies give rise to paradigms (patterns of thought) referred to as the positivist and interpretivist paradigms. Before we look at the characteristics of positivism and interpretivism, we need to consider exactly what we mean by a paradigm and how we have arrived at a position whereby researchers generally associate themselves, rightly or wrongly, with one particular paradigm or the other. This is important, as we need to be able to articulate how our view has informed our subsequent decisions about research design to those who share our interests and are in turn, interested in our research findings.

Research paradigms

A paradigm is a set of assumptions, concepts, values and practices constituting a view of reality. In terms of research a paradigm represents a view shared by a scientific community about how we can come to know the essence of things (*ontology*), and how we can come to know what is true, and what is false (*epistemology*). Over time, scientific communities have come to hold a common set of assumptions and values and to follow certain rules in pursuit of solutions to problems in the real world. For example, doctors working in coronary care (a scientific community) wanted to know if the changes in coronary care in the mid-1980s to mid-1990s had resulted in better outcomes or endpoints for patients (Capewell *et al.*, 1999). The assumption made by this scientific community of doctors is that it is possible to answer the question by comparing different population groups undergoing different treatments across different periods. The data were analysed using statistical tests and indicated that later treatment modalities improved patients' outcomes, although other changes such as economic success may account for some of the positive outcomes seen in some patient populations. The paradigm underpinning this research is positivism.

Positivism

Positivists believe that the goal of science is to uncover the truth. Consequently, a positivist would view science as a means of getting at the truth in order to understand the world well enough to predict and control it. Stereotypically, sci-

3

entists are depicted wearing white coats and based in laboratories. This image was certainly true in the past, supported by popular imagery such as television and film. Positivistic scientists are interested in observing what can be seen (phenomena), describing what is seen, and measuring what is seen. Knowledge of anything beyond the observed, described, and measured is impossible to the positivist. Taking this a step further, a positivist would argue that those things not directly observed – for example, thoughts, feelings and emotions – are not legitimate subjects for study. A fundamental positivist would argue that what cannot be measured is irrelevant. Positivists believe empiricism (the pursuit of knowledge by observation and experiment) to be central to scientific endeavour. Hence positivistic research is usually of an experimental design and uses quantitative approaches to data collection (we return to this later).

Post-positivism

In recent times (since the mid 20th century) thinking about science has undergone a marked shift, with a rejection of the positivistic view that science works through observation and experiment and that this is distinctly different from how everyday life is experienced. In an era now defined as post-positivism, scientists do not view scientific reasoning and common sense reasoning as mutually exclusive but as part of the same process: namely, an attempt to make sense of the world. Scientific research relies on results which are verifiable, accurate and consistent. Although common sense reasoning does not always proceed in a systematic way, it is often underpinned by observation and measurement. When thinking about everyday healthcare practice you will be able to recall occasions when you knew your patient's condition had deteriorated long before any clinical observations confirmed your suspicions. This is intuitive practice, and while not underpinned by evidence in the scientific sense, it is based on observations of similar patients with similar conditions over considerable periods. Indeed, Patricia Benner's classic work recognised that nurses arrive at an understanding of patient care over time through not only a sound educational base, but also from a multitude of experiences (Benner, 1984). The most common form of post-positivist thinking is a philosophy known as critical realism, which attempts to reconcile the position taken by the positivist and that taken by the interpretivist.

Critical realism

Critical realism recognises that observation is always fallible and prone to error; therefore theory can always be revised. The critical realist is critical of our ability to know reality with any degree of certainty. Of importance to the critical realist is the idea of holding fast to an attempt to get it right about reality rather than uncovering the truth, simply because we may never know the truth for sure. A critical realist will attempt to use multiple methods (triangulation) to observe and measure reality in an effort to understand what is happening in the real world. These varying methods may have different types of error within them; you may have your view of the world based on your experience and I will have mine. For example, we may watch the same football match and experience it in different ways depending on which team we support; I believe the goal to be offside, you believe it to be onside. The goal is disallowed, so technically my perception is correct and yours is incorrect. While your perception will not change, you may come to understand my perspective, recognising it as constructed by my own experience. Critical realism allows multiple fallible sources to get a better view of what is going on by acknowledging that all observations including those of scientists are theory laden and biased by experience. At this point you may well be asking how we can conduct research in any objective way if we allow multiple sources to inform our understanding of what is occurring (the phenomenon being studied), especially since these have been shown to be very different. A critical realist would argue that objectivity is not exclusive to an individual but rather belongs to a social group. Objectivity is what we strive for when we criticise each other's work. In this sense, we may never achieve true objectivity, but as a community of truth seekers we can approach objectivity through scrutiny. Those theories that survive scrutiny are theories we can be most confident in. For example, if we listen to our patients who consistently tell us they fear going into hospital because of the risk of infection we can develop a theory that patients are concerned about the risk of hospital-acquired infection. The actual risk may be low in terms of total number of patients admitted to hospital. However, anxiety and stress are known to lower resistance, making it more likely that anxious patients will be less resistant to infection. Using multiple sources of evidence, some of which may be fallible, allows for theory to be generated; for example, patients whose fears and anxieties around hospital-acquired infection are recognised and addressed are less likely to succumb to infection in the hospital setting.

Interpretivism

As we have shown, the positivist researcher places emphasis on explanation, prediction, and control. Enquiry using a positivistic approach answers questions that readily lend themselves to numerical measurement; for example, how many nursing students use the library facilities at the weekend, and during which hours. These types of question are important, as we need to be able to predict library usage in the future and to ensure that supply can meet demand. Important questions around the provision of healthcare services lend themselves to positivistic enquiry; for example, the length of time that patients may be waiting for healthcare services. Answers to these questions are important in order to ensure that patients receive the care they need in a timely fashion in the most cost-effective manner (you can think of many more important questions that lend themselves to this type if enquiry). What positivist approaches to enquiry cannot tell us is how individuals, be they student or patient, or indeed individuals in any social situation, perceive, interpret and make sense of the situation. To continue with the earlier examples, we might also want to know what students think about the library weekend opening times, how this relates to their view of the university as a whole, and how it helps or hinders their overall study experience. Similarly, we need to know how patients feel about waiting for healthcare services, how this influences their experience of health and illness, and how they make sense of these experiences now and the likely impact of this on future health behaviour. Collecting numerical data to help predict and control will not shed light on these important questions. For this, we need a different approach, namely an interpretive approach to enquiry.

The interpretive approach to enquiry links with philosophy and the human sciences. Researchers adopting an interpretivist approach think of individuals as existing not in isolation, but as inseparable from the wider context of their everyday lives. Students at university are not separate from the wider social context in which they live; they bring the context of their lives with them, and their experience of university occurs within this context. Each student will have a unique university experience, while at the same time sharing similar experiences with other students. Similarly, patients bring the wider context of their lives with them to the healthcare setting, and this shapes and colours their experience of health and illness.

Social scientists are concerned for the most part with understanding the unique world in which the individual lives. While the social scientist may use numerical data to inform their enquiry, emphasis is placed on understanding the world of the 'other' rather than explaining that world. Social scientists use interpretivist approaches to gain access to an individual's experience and perception of reality. Social scientists are interested in qualitative expression, rather than quantitative measurement. Consequently, interpretivist researchers use qualitative approaches to data collection.

In summary, we have looked at philosophies of research as a starting point for thinking about how we might undertake research to underpin our practice: an important part of a nurse's role and responsibilities to patients, which is as important as updating clinical knowledge. We began by thinking about how we might come to know the social world in which we live. There are generally two traditions, with opposing views, namely positivism, with its emphasis on the observable and objective way of knowing the social world, and interpretivism, or a subjective view of knowing the social world. Whichever view is subscribed to on a personal level, the key point is to think about the research question (i.e. what do we want to know?), and to design the research study in a way that best enables the question to be answered. For example, a researcher seeking to understand student nurses' experience of using the library would design a study grounded in interpretivism whereby it is possible to come to know what it is like to use the library from the students' perspective. On the other hand, a researcher wishing to know peak usage time for the library would design a study within the positivist paradigm and observe students using the library during certain times of the day. Both are useful pieces of research, but for different reasons and for different audiences. It is useful for library staff to know how students experience the library, so that they can facilitate improvements. However, if the question is one of how to make best use of available resources, a different audience will be interested in the results, namely those responsible for resourcing the library and capital expenditure. What is suitable for one research study may not be suitable for another, depending on the question and the targeted audience for the research findings.

The research question

The research process begins when there is a problem in need of a solution, with the aim being to design a research study that will enable the problem to be solved. This is true irrespective of the preferred methodology, be it quantitative or qualitative. Identifying research problems in healthcare is relatively simple, as most of us have worked in the field in some capacity. Consequently, exposure and experience of healthcare situations means we are best placed to identify problems of interest to the real world of healthcare practice. Often the identification of a research problem arises from a disagreement or discussion. For example, how nursing care should be organised, how health services should be delivered, or what treatments and care patients require, or desire. The researcher then translates these disagreements or discussions into a researchable question and proceeds to design a research study, using the most appropriate methodology to address the research question. In general, research ideas and questions arise from existing theories or previous research. Similarly, research questions in nursing can arise from everyday nursing practice, past nursing research or nursing theory.

One of the most fruitful areas for research ideas is everyday nursing practice. Practitioners continually have to make decisions about how to organise care, when to alert medical staff to a change in a patient's condition, and more often these days how to make best use of available resources. Practitioners will be constantly observing and reflecting on their practice and the practice of others and thinking about how best to solve clinical and practice problems. Situations and experiences such as these, and many others you can think of, can be turned into research questions with the aim of improving practice for the benefit of patients and clients.

Previous research studies are another source of research ideas and questions since they often recommend further research in a subject. An interesting feature of research is that it tends to generate more questions than it answers. In addition, from reviewing and analysing research articles as a student you may have found issues in the published research, which are problematic. In this case, your critique may be a good starting place to propose further research, which in turn adds to the body of nursing knowledge.

The necessity to test theory or to build theory is another source of research ideas and/or questions. Theory is an explanation of how a phenomenon operates and why. Theory serves the purpose of making sense out of current knowledge by integrating and summarising what is currently known. Theory building goes beyond what is currently known and attempts to suggest new relationships and make new predictions. New research studies can confirm or disconfirm nursing theory.

Identifying a research idea or problem does not mean that this will be the exact focus of your research study, as the issue may have already been researched sufficiently for theory to become accepted practice. Alternatively, you may have identified a broad topic area from experience or observations of everyday practice, from previous research, or existing theory that now requires a different or innovative approach to investigation. Identification of the research topic is the beginning of the sequential process that leads to the generation of the research question and culminates in the design of the research study. Refining the research question and designing the research study requires a review of the research literature.

The literature review

Once the research topic has been identified, the next stage is to find out what is already known about the area to be investigated. The aim here is to refine the topic into a researchable question, to ensure the research study will add to what is known about the issue, and to avoid repeating the limitations of previous research studies.

Reading and reviewing the literature to find out what is known about a subject can involve a number of sources, for example previous research studies published in academic journals, anecdotal accounts of practice, or textbooks and documentary sources. Reference can also be made to sources such as radio, television, audiovisual media such as slides, and photographs. Online databases are a good source of information, as are Internet sources. However, the researcher should exercise caution and needs to maintain a degree of scepticism regarding the validity and reliability of online sources until the quality of the material can be verified. Cross-checking and referring to sources other than the Internet, for example published papers, are ways of doing this.

The literature review also serves the purpose of providing a rationale for a research study. Researchers may claim the reason for undertaking research is that little or no research exists in a particular area. In this case, the literature review provides evidence that this is in fact the case, with literature cited that relates to the proposed study but drawn from a broader subject area. The researchers are then able to justify the need for more focused research. A further reason for undertaking a literature review is to provide a context for the proposed research. In this case, the literature review locates the current study within the context of what is already known in the subject area.

The value of information to a given research study depends on whether it is a primary or secondary source. Original literature is a primary source: for example, a government report or textbook, or where the researcher has access to the original publication of a research study. Secondary sources are those where a person other than the person who undertook the original research reports on research. Both sources are useful. However, it is important where possible to draw on primary sources, as secondary sources may misinterpret, misreport or distort the original literature. Where it is not possible to acquire the primary source, secondary sources are useful in shedding light on or conveying the essence of the original source. The researcher must make it clear, using recognised referencing techniques, whether sources of material are primary or secondary, and should as far as possible avoid over-using secondary sources.

The extent of a literature review is dependent on the target audience. For example, the review might be undertaken as part of original research for a programme of study such as a Master's degree or a PhD. In these circumstances, the extent of the literature review is constrained by convention. In externally funded research projects the extent of the literature review may be determined by available resources and the requirements of funding bodies. Researchers will not be able to write about all the literature on a subject and will need to make a judgement regarding what *must* be included, what *could* be included, and what can reasonably be *omitted*. In most cases there will be literature that is integral to the proposed research, is deemed a classic text, and whose omission would seriously affect the integrity of the review. In most literature reviews, the researchers refer to the scope of the review, indicating the period covered by the review, the countries covered by the review and any other distinguishing features of the review.

We note here that some research studies consist entirely of a systematic review of the literature, whereby the researcher reviews and evaluates what is already published in a given area. Systematic reviews are an accepted research approach and can serve as research in their own right or as an integral part of the literature review for a new study.

Research methodologies

A research paradigm is a worldview including philosophical and socio-political issues, whereas a research methodology is a general approach to scientific inquiry involving preferences for broad components of the research process (Teddlie and Tashakkori, 2009). Research methodology refers to the principles guiding the researcher's choice of strategy and procedure for undertaking research. A researcher chooses a methodological approach to carrying out the research, based on a preferred research philosophy. As we have seen, research philosophy is a set of beliefs about how we can come to know the world, namely positivist or interpretivist. Positivistic methodologies are quantitative in nature, whereas interpretivist methodologies are qualitative in nature. Methodology is a general approach to a scientific inquiry.

Quantitative methodology

Quantitative methodology is used in research studies in which the data are analysed numerically. Relatively large data sets are used, which are representative of the broad population being studied. Statistical tools are used to analyse the data and these are often complex in order to given additional meaning to the research findings. Statistical tests are used to describe data in a meaningful way or to infer from the study population what may pertain to the whole of that population. Quantitative approaches to research are useful in understanding trends and are used in the field of public health to look at underlying patterns of disease and to predict future requirements for the provision of healthcare services. Quantitative research will not explain or shed light on how individuals think about healthcare services, or indeed what they prefer to be available. Without this information, healthcare planners may make inappropriate choices for service provision to the detriment of patient satisfaction.

Qualitative methodology

Qualitative methodology is used in research which seeks to understand the individual's point of view. Large data sets are not necessary, as the aim is not to generalise or infer from the findings to the whole of the population for that study. Rather, the aim is to understand from the individual respondent how the phenomenon is experienced. Sample size may be relatively small in qualitative research, depending on the method of data collection. Data from qualitative research are not subject to statistical tests, as respondents usually tell of their experiences, or feelings, in their own words. Common methods for collecting qualitative data are interviews and focus groups, transcribed verbatim (word for word).

Conclusion

In this chapter we have looked at research philosophy and research paradigms. We have learnt that researchers usually hold a philosophical position about how we can come to know the social world around us. The view taken is, on the one hand, that the social world is understood only through knowledge from direct observation and measurement, or on the other hand, that the social world can be understood through knowledge from accounts of individual experience.

We considered the centrality of both the research question and the literature review in decisions about research design. We then looked at research methodology and learnt that researchers who come from a scientific background usually adhere to the first philosophical position and will therefore hold a set of assumptions, concepts, values and practices consistent with the positivist paradigm. These researchers generally undertake research using quantitative methods, which involve collecting numerical data. In contrast, researchers coming from a social science background, including health and social care, will more than likely adhere to the second philosophical position, and therefore hold a set of assumptions, concepts, values and practices consistent with the interpretivist paradigm. These researchers generally undertake research using qualitative methods, which involve collecting descriptive data. In the next chapter, we provide an overview of qualitative research methods.

Further reading

Dyson, S. and Brown, B. (2006) *Social Theory and Applied Health Research.* Open University Press, Berkshire.
Lincoln, Y. and Guba, E. (1985) *Naturalistic Inquiry.* Sage, London.
Midgeley, M. (2001) *Science and Poetry.* Routledge, London.

CHAPTER 2

Qualitative research: an overview of methods

Introduction

Qualitative research encompasses a wide range of methodologies and methods. However, all qualitative work is interpretive in nature. A key aspect of qualitative research is a reliance on unstructured information to answer key questions. In this sense, qualitative research does not rely on statistics or numbers. Consequently the methods used to gather data (information) are usually interviews (structured, semi-structured and unstructured), focus groups and analysis of documentary evidence including diaries, video clips, oral histories and testimonials; indeed any unstructured information. Any method of data collection that seeks to answer the 'why' and not the 'how' of its subject is more than likely to be qualitative in nature.

Take as an example a qualitative study conducted by Ashing-Giwa *et al.* (2004) to investigate the breast cancer experiences of African American, Asian American, Latina and Caucasian breast cancer survivors. One hundred and two breast cancers survivors from different ethnic groups participated in focus groups exploring differences in types of treatment, quality of life and ongoing concerns after treatment. Through invitation, the women talked about their experiences and the researchers were able to show that there are indeed differences in treatments offered to women from different ethnic groups. Women of colour are less likely to receive adjuvant therapies, including radiation and chemotherapy, and more likely to receive mastectomies. Furthermore, while all women experience similar concerns, for example recurrence of the cancer and worries about family, body image and sexual health, women of colour reported their spiritual beliefs and practices to be central to their coping. The results of this qualitative study, whereby the women were given a 'voice' and an opportunity to talk about individual experiences of breast cancer, provided invaluable information for healthcare providers and future survivors of breast cancer about the impact of culture on survivorship, in ways that a quantitative study would not.

There are a number of approaches to conducting qualitative research. While these are all interpretivist in nature, the approaches taken to data collection and subsequent data analysis are different. We now consider some approaches to qualitative research widely used in the social sciences, including the health-care professions.

Qualitative methods

Ethnography

A good place to begin to think about different approaches to qualitative research is to look first at ethnography, for reasons that ethnography is considered the oldest of the qualitative approaches. The purpose of ethnography is to provide a detailed description of everyday life events or 'thick description', and for this reason much qualitative research is ethnographic in nature. Ethnography is the research method of anthropology and as such can trace its history back to the Greeks and Romans who described their travels in detail (thick description). In its purest sense, ethnography is a description of the people or a writing of a culture (Holloway, 1997).

Ethnography is both research process and research outcome, in that the researcher conducts an ethnographic study, but also produces an interpretation of the culture under investigation. *Culture*, used here in its broadest sense, refers to a system of knowledge shared by a relatively large group of people. Ethnographers may study many different cultures, for example organisational culture, business culture, cultural practice in nursing, cultural practice in midwifery or culture in nurse education. What the ethnographer is concerned with, whatever the culture studied, is the web of meaning (Geertz, 1973) or the cultural constructions in which the members of that particular culture live. The ultimate aim of the ethnographer is to observe, record, analyse and then interpret the information collected (data), to gain the meaning of the culture itself, with the ultimate goal of initiating dialogues between cultures. Imagine an ethnographic study which aimed to describe in detail the cultural practices of nurses working in accident and emergency (A&E) and to make sense of those practices as understood by the nurses themselves. The ethnographic researcher, immersed in the world of A&E, is best placed to observe, analyse and interpret what it means to work under pressure, to meet the targets, and to ensure patients do not remain in A&E longer than four hours from admission to transfer (DoH, 2000). Ethnography, with its emphasis on the '*emic*' or insider's point of view, is able to generate a cultural understanding of A&E practice, thus enabling critical categories and meanings to emerge rather than imposing these by using approaches which are essentially *'etic'* or from an outsider's perspective. In summary, an ethnographic exploration is one developed through close exploration of a number of sources of data, usually collected over time, on which the researcher comes to rely to develop a cultural frame of reference.

Hammersley (1990) provides us with a summary of the features of ethnographic research that are useful in helping us recognise ethnographic research:

- People's behaviour is studied in everyday contexts, rather than under experimental conditions created by the researcher.
- Data are gathered from a range of sources, but usually from observation and relatively informal conversations.
- The approach to data collection is unstructured and does not normally follow a detailed plan set up at the beginning; nor are the categories used for interpreting what people say and do predetermined or fixed. This does not mean the research is unsystematic, rather that initial data are collected in as raw a form as possible, and on as wide a front as is feasible.
- The focus is usually a single setting or group, of relatively small scale.
- Data analysis involves interpretation of the meanings and functions of human actions and mainly takes the form of verbal descriptions and explanations, with quantifications and statistical analysis, if present, taking a subordinate role at most.

There are a number of options available to ethnographic researchers in terms of collecting data. However, what is required is a commitment to getting as close to the subject observed as possible. It is essential to collect data in a natural setting, and to report these data in a factual and descriptive manner. The points of view of the recipients are integral, and an absolute commitment to accurate and true reporting is essential to ethnographic research. Once the rules of good ethnographic research are observed, the researcher can design the study and subsequent methods for collecting data in a way that best serves the situation. There are usually two approaches taken to data collection in ethnography, both of which involve observation. However, observation is either participant or non-participant depending on the context in which the research is taking place, access to the participants, ethical issues and available resources. In addition, within the decision to choose either participant or non-participant observation, an ethnographic researcher will have to decide on the extent of the participation or non-participation, for example, the researcher immersed in a culture or observer of a culture. Alternatively, the researcher may take a position that is somewhere between the two.

Phenomenology

In Chapter 1 we looked at the philosophical positions taken by researchers when attempting to think about the social world in which we live. We considered the scientific or positivist approach, which seeks to understand the world through recording as evidence only that which is directly observed, and discounting all that cannot be directly observed. In contrast to this view is phenomenology, which by its very nature is essentially relative and subjective. We now move on to consider phenomenology in detail and discuss why researchers might choose a phenomenological approach when undertaking qualitative research.

Phenomenology has overlaps with other approaches to qualitative research, in particular ethnography, which we have previously considered. However, phenomenology is unique in that the point of phenomenology, unlike ethnography, is to describe, rather than explain. It is important here to note that most researchers using a phenomenological approach do explain their findings as integral to undertaking research with a purpose. We will return to this later.

Pure phenomenological research is free from hypotheses and preconceptions. Husserl (1970), considered the father of phenomenology, talks about the concept of the life world as a key concept and focus of investigation for phenomenology, where the life world comprises the world of objects around us as we perceive them and our experience of our self, body and relationships. Life world is the world that is lived and experienced and takes place before we think about it or put it into language, i.e. before we have time to reflect on it. Merleau-Ponty (1962, p. 10), another key figure in the development of phenomenology explains, 'man is in the world and only in that world does he know himself'.

There are numerous variants of phenomenological philosophy, for example *hermeneutic phenomenology*, which highlights the researchers role and interpretations in the research, *heuristic phenomenology*, which highlights the place of self-reflection in producing a creative account of the participants lived experience, and *relational research* approaches, where attention is paid to the researcher's own journey (Finlay, 2008). The particular approach taken to conducting phenomenological research is dependent on the researcher's philosophical values, theoretical position, and methodological preferences. However, broadly speaking phenomenology is flexible and allows for a wide range of investigations into issues in health and social care. For example, Dyson *et al.* (2008) used a phenomenological approach to investigate the lived experiences of South Asian nursing students on pre-registration programmes in a UK university. Using this approach enabled the researchers to describe the world of the student in the particular context of being South Asian. The researchers came to know the world as lived by the student and were able to make recommendations for nurse educators in relation to supporting students from particular ethnic groups as they attempt to traverse an essentially ethnocentric curriculum.

Finlay's (2008) features of phenomenological research are useful in helping us recognise phenomenological research:

- Phenomenology asks what this kind of experience is like.
- What does this experience mean?
- Phenomenological researchers help participants to express their world as directly as possible.
- Phenomenological researchers assist participants to reveal the dimensions of the lived world, so that the lived world is revealed.
- Meanings uncovered by the researcher emerge out of the way the researcher poses the questions. In particular, the researcher brackets or suspends previously held assumptions about the phenomenon in order to be open to the phenomenon as it appears.
- The researcher aims to be open and to see the world as the participant sees it.

In summary, most research in the field of health and social care is not phenomenological in the true sense of the word. Researchers in health and social care more often than not use issues of concern for practitioners as their starting point. By this, I mean that the researchers already have a preconceived idea, if not a hypothesis, about the phenomenon under investigation. Very few researchers in health and social care do not take a view on what is happening in their field of practice. As such, it is usually the methods of data collection that are phenomenological, rather than the overall philosophical approach to the research. Nonetheless, phenomenological methods of data collection are extremely effective in prioritising and centralising the perspectives or voices of those affected by a given situation. In cases where these voices are marginalised, for example a minority group or underrepresented group, phenomenology, with its focus on the experiences and perceptions of the individuals concerned, can be extremely powerful in challenging the assumptions on which many structures in health and social care are founded.

Phenomenological research is carried out with relatively small numbers of participants, as is the case with all qualitative research where size does not matter. However, the ability of the research to add to the body of evidence about a particular phenomenon may be limited when small numbers of participants are included. In pure phenomenology this does not matter, as the point is to describe the phenomenon from the individual's perspective and not necessarily to infer from the study to the broader population. However, in research in health and social care the point is often to make recommendations for future practice. Therefore, while phenomenological research can be robust in uncovering factors and their influence on individual cases it needs to be tentative in suggesting their extent in relation to the wider population from which the participants are drawn (Lester, 1999). This is a feature of all qualitative research and involves a move away from the concept of generalisability of research findings to a more appropriate discussion of transferability of research findings. We will consider this is more detail in a later chapter.

Grounded theory

Grounded theory is a particular approach to qualitative enquiry which puts constant comparison of data at its heart. Barney Glaser and Anselm Strauss originally developed the method in 1967. In grounded theory the process begins with a research situation whereby the task of the researcher is to understand the roles of the players/actors in that situation. Data are collected from observations, conversations, and/or interviews. Data from interviews (or other data) are compared to interviews (or other data), and data from observations (or other data) are compared to observations (or other data). After each episode of data collection, the researcher engages in a process of note taking as issues emerge. Constant comparison is central to the process and theory tends to emerge quickly. The results of the comparisons of the note taking, written as codes, help the researchers to formulate categories and sub-categories, very much like themes and sub-themes. As this process of coding proceeds, the researcher begins to develop theoretical propositions, for example about links between categories or about a core category or one which is central to the study. The links between categories, sub-categories and core categories provide the theory.

A key feature of grounded theory is the notes the researchers write to themselves, which act as memos. As the data collection and coding proceeds, the notes and memos build up.

In grounded theory, the sample is added to theoretically. This is a purposive approach (we will look at this in more detail later) which increases the diversity of the sample by allowing the researcher to look for different properties. For example, if a core category becomes saturated with data, then the researcher ceases data collection from this sample and moves onto the next category or sub-category. Data collection continues, increasing the sample as necessary until no new data emerges. When the process is complete, i.e. all categories and sub-categories are saturated, the researcher can move to the next step, which is sorting, whereby all memos (notes to self) accumulated are grouped in the order that best allows theory to become clear.

In grounded theory, literature is accessed as part of the process of data collection, coding, note taking and memo writing, and not generally undertaken as a predetermined search before data collection commences. This method allows literature to be accessed as necessary or as the need arises from emerging theory, which is grounded in the data. Glaser saw this as key to the method and argued that most research, including qualitative methodology, is actually hypothesis testing.

Dick (2005) provides a useful framework for identifying the essential steps in the process of grounded theory:

- The aim of grounded theory is to discover the theory implicit in the data.
- Grounded theory does not test a hypothesis.
- Grounded theory sets out to find what theory accounts for the research situation as it is.
- Data collection, note taking, coding and memoing occur simultaneously.
- Sorting occurs when all categories are saturated.
- Writing occurs after sorting.
- Theory is emergent – discovered in the data.

In summary, grounded theory is an emergent method. By this, we mean data collection begins as soon as a research situation arises and not at a later point and literature is accessed as it becomes relevant. Glaser (1978) suggests an alternative approach is to read broadly as a background to the research rather than reading the literature most closely associated with the subject of the research, as the latter approach may constrain coding and memoing. When using grounded theory the researcher needs to carefully seek disconfirming evidence as theory develops. In so doing, the grounded theorist is responsive to the data and draws on relevant literature as a simultaneous part of the research process.

Action research

Action research is fundamentally a research method aimed at changing practice. Action research works with practitioners and/or community members. Research findings, used immediately, continually develop and change practice. Action research undertaken *with* participants, rather than *to* them, always involves a collaborative and partnership approach to collecting data.

Action research is often credited to Kurt Lewin, a Prussian psychologist who later emigrated to the USA and worked mostly in the field of group dynamics. Lewin developed the concept of 'rational social management', which sought to combine experimental approaches with social action. Lewin believed in proceeding in a spiral of steps, each one composed of a circle of planning, action and fact finding about the result of the action. This approach characterises action research as we have come to know it and is an extremely powerful means of collaborating with practitioners to bring about positive change.

It should be noted that for action research to achieve its intended aim to 'improve and involve' (Carr and Kemmis, 1986, p. 165), equal partnership, whereby practitioners are deemed co-researchers, is essential. This partnership will usually see practitioners collecting data about their situation, finding strategies to solve the problem and converting the strategies into action (Holloway, 1997). The original researcher or person outside the practice arena may act as a catalyst for change and facilitate analysis of the situation by the practitioners, who are then empowered to instigate the necessary changes.

Action research involves the steps of planning, acting, observing/evaluating and reflecting, and these steps are integral to the design of the research and taken with full participation of all stakeholders in the research. Figure 2.1 shows how the steps form a continuous process of planning, acting, observing/evaluating and reflecting to ensure each action or change can be addressed if it does not meet the needs of those who will be affected by it.

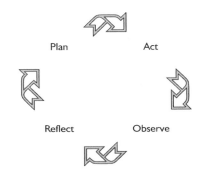

Plan   Act

Reflect   Observe

Figure 2.1 Steps in action research.

In recent years, action research has come to be used to empower disenfranchised groups and to challenge the social structures that create such power imbalances. Action research, when used in this way, is known as participatory action research and is premised on the notion of co-researchers working together as equal partners trying out various actions, observing those actions, evaluating and reflecting on the effectiveness of the actions in improving practice. This process allows the co-researchers to analyse the situation they are in, to develop solutions to real world problems, and to become empowered to bring about positive change. In situations where professional practice is dictated by policies outside the control or influence of the practitioners themselves, participatory action research is a powerful research method to provide the evidence base for changing practice. However, it should be noted that the problems must be those identified by the practitioners themselves and not suggested or imposed by the organisation. In cases where the issues are not those identified by practitioners then true participatory action research is not undertaken and the method is used to maintain the status quo or to instigate change against the wishes of the practitioners.

Wadsworth (1998) provides us with an explanation of participatory action research:

- Participatory action research consciously problematises an existing action or practice and defines who is problematising it and why.
- Participatory action research consciously names the problem, raises questions about the problem, and focuses on the need to answer the question.
- Participatory action research is planned and deliberate about commencing the process of inquiry and consciously considers all those who need to be involved in the inquiry.
- Participatory action research is systematic and rigorous in its efforts to get answers to the problematic action or practice.
- Participatory action research carefully documents and records each action taken to address the problem and what people think about each action taken, in ways that are relevant and meaningful to all interested parties.
- Participatory action research is intensive, comprehensive and cautious, before jumping to conclusions.
- Participatory action research attempts to develop deep understanding and more useful and powerful theory about the problem in order to improve action or practice.
- Changing action or practice is fundamental to participatory action research and is followed by further participatory action research to investigate the changed action or practice.

In summary, action research (and participatory action research in particular), considers it critical to the success of the inquiry that the question posed in the first place is one that is relevant and useful to those affected by. Participatory action research considers where the problems have come from and insists that new actions or practices arising from the inquiry are tested in action. In participatory action research a cyclical, rather than a linear, model is used, which starts with reflection on action, and proceeds to new action, which is then further researched until all those participating in delivering the service agree best practice.

Feminist research

Feminist research studies the social context of women's lives from a standpoint that essentially views society as patriarchal and male dominated. The aim of feminist research is to enlighten society about the taken-for-granted sexist practices and gender blindness of governments and most community practices that have led to the displacement of women, ignoring women, and often the silencing of women. Feminist research is research by women for women, with the intention of making women visible, raising their consciousness and empowering them (Holloway, 1997).

Feminist research traces its roots in feminist theory. Cott (1987) delineates modern feminist theory from its antecedents, particularly the struggle for suffrage. A distinction may be drawn between the women's movement prior to suffrage, which was primarily about the woman as a universal entity, and the post-suffrage movement, which was more concerned with social differentiation. In recent times feminist theory has dealt with issues such as women's condition as a social construct, gender identity, and relationships within and between genders. Feminist research is based on this body of critical theory built over time. As you would expect, feminist research is, by its very nature, critical and emancipatory, perceiving reality, science and research in this context.

The methods employed by feminist researchers generally fit best with the interpretivist paradigm, as the assumption underpinning feminist research is of the world as a socially constructed place. However, feminists do and have used quantitative methods if the nature of the inquiry requires them to do so. This recourse to a mixed methods approach in feminist research has caused some consternation for feminists who believe the true feminist position rejects any form of positivism. For postmodern feminist researchers a more liberal approach allows for and requires that the methods of data collection be dictated by the inquiry itself. All feminist research seeks to be value-free and to place the interests of women as central to its endeavour.

Sarantakos (2005) provides us with a clear and concise guide to the principles on which feminist research is premised:

- Women have been marginalised.
- Male superiority is perpetuated despite policies, assurances, and political promises.
- That males and females are considered physically and emotionally different, with men being considered superior.
- That there is still a long way to go to establish gender equality.
- That the relationship between researcher and researched requires serious reconsideration.

In summary, feminist research takes as its focus the experiences and perceptions of women. As Holloway (1997) succinctly puts it, feminist approaches do not prescribe methods of analysing research, but suggest ways of thinking about it. However, the commonality in all feminist research is the positioning of the 'feminine' as central, with the intention of making the often invisible woman visible. While some feminist researchers argue for a distinct and separate feminist research methodology, others take a more liberal view and argue that feminist research is research that aims to change the status of women in society, to redress the balance, and to study women. In this sense, feminist research, irrespective of methodology, is research conducted on women, for women, and by women.

Narrative research

Narrative research epitomises the qualitative approach to research perhaps more than any other methodology, being naturalistic, phenomenological, ethnographic and inherently subjective (Polkinghorne, 1988). The core of narrative research is relativism, rather than absolute truths, in other words an acceptance on the part of the researcher of the existence of more than one reality or truth. This fundamental aspect of narrative research makes it the ideal approach for researchers in health and social care who wish to understand the life stories of individuals experiencing physical and psychological ill health, and indeed for all research which seeks to understand the life trajectories of individuals. Take for example research carried out by Dyson (2005), which examined the life experiences of Zimbabwean nursing students studying in the UK. A narrative approach was employed to understand the life histories of students leaving their homeland to live, study, and in most cases work in another country, and the meaning they attributed to these experiences. A narrative approach allowed stories to be told in the students' voice. For the first time since arriving in the UK, students were able to share previously untold aspects of their lives, including what it is like to leave their country of birth, find accommodation and begin studying in the UK, at the same time as remitting monies home for families who needed help and support to remain in Zimbabwe. Narrative research has the potential to draw attention to the voices of marginalised people, often silenced through circumstances beyond their control. In this sense, narrative research is both powerful and sensitive in ways that other methodologies are not. Consider the case of asylum seekers fleeing from countries where life is made unsustainable by governments hostile to dissent of any kind. On arrival in the UK, asylum seekers are detained until the Home Office hears their cases, which can take up to two years (Cleave, 2009). Narrative research is especially sensitive to the unique characteristics of human existence and is therefore ideal for research which aims to come as close as possible to the meaning of subjective experience. Narrative research enables social scientists to study people rather than variables.

Narrative research is not without its challenges. The first of these is the amount of material generated from narrative interviewing. Respondents, invited to tell their stories in their own words and in their own context, often include a personal time frame. Narrative interviewing requires the respondent to cede the floor to the teller, in other words to step back and allow the respondent to take over the conversation. This is essential, as story telling is the focus of the research and the story itself is the object of the investigation. The second challenge lies with the analysis. Narrative is subtle, complex and difficult to interpret (Riessman, 1993). Accounts of stories told by respondents are often multifaceted, and can be at odds with the researcher's firmly held views of the social world, including what the researcher thinks they know of the world of the respondent. To complicate matters further, notions of reality and identity are constructions that take place on different levels, within a certain context and in a certain language, and much can be lost in translation. Nevertheless, in spite of the challenges of using a narrative approach, people do live the events and affairs of their lives in a storied way. What we think we know of another's life is more often than not far removed from the 'truth' as that person experiences it. Narrative research allows us to make sense of experiences by casting them in a story and gives an insight into the intensely human realm of value (Riessman, 1993).

Riessman (1993) suggests that all narrative research:

- aims to study people by listening
- the act of listening implies sensitivity to the unique characteristics of human existence
- is guided by a core of consensus regarding facts, traits and processes, about which different subjective accounts agree
- aims towards novel observational experience
- creates new views about man's social world

Narratives are stories told by individuals about their condition, work, or lives. Narratives have existed for centuries in the forms of diaries, oral histories, or travellers' tales. The systematic collection of stories, whatever their form, is known as narrative research. The narrative approach, although not without its challenges, is especially useful for studying transformations and transitions in individuals' lives and is therefore a powerful methodological approach for researching aspects of health and illness (Holloway, 1997).

Conclusion

In this chapter we have considered what we mean by qualitative research. Qualitative research, founded on the belief that the social world, or world inhabited by individuals, can only be known by asking questions of individuals about how they are affected by a particular issue: what impact the issue has on their lives, what sense they make of the issue and how they would change their situation if they could. Qualitative research is not interested in knowing the extent of the issue, or the range of issues. In this sense, qualitative research fits within the interpretivist paradigm, which focuses on human beings and the way they interpret and make sense of reality.

We then considered a number of approaches to conducting qualitative research including ethnography, phenomenology, grounded theory, action research, feminist research and narrative research. These approaches are not exhaustive but will enable you to recognise qualitative research and the different approaches qualitative researchers take to their work, based on the kinds of questions they seek to answer. In the next chapter, we look at strategies for selecting participants, and methods for collecting and analysing data in qualitative research.

Further reading

Bryman, A. (2001) *Social Research Methods*. Oxford University Press. Oxford.

Holloway, I. (1997) *Basic Concepts for Qualitative Research*. Blackwell Science, Oxford.

Parahoo, K. (2006). *Nursing Research. Principles, Process and Issues*, 2nd edn. Palgrave MacMillan, Hampshire.

CHAPTER 3

Qualitative research: data collection and analysis

Introduction

Methods generally employed in qualitative research may vary. However, the most commonly used approaches to data collection, include direct observation, interviews or focus groups, analysis of texts and documents and of recorded speech such as video and audio tapes (Pope and Mays, 2000). The key feature of all these data collection techniques is the emphasis on the actual events and the verbalisation of events by those experiencing them, rather than on numbers. In this sense, as Pope and Mays (2000, p. 7) suggest, these methods (at least on one level) are those we use in everyday situations as we try to make sense of the world – 'we watch what is going on, ask questions of each other and try to comprehend the social world we live in'. Before we look in detail at methods of data collection in qualitative research, we need to think about who we need to collect data from in order to answer our research question.

Sampling in qualitative research

In qualitative research, it is not possible to collect data from everyone in a given community or population due to the methods used, for example interviews and focus groups. Therefore qualitative researchers choose a sample or subset of a population using a specific strategy to ensure that the sample is representative of the population they wish to study. The sampling strategy is guided by the research question, the research aims and objectives and to a certain extent the resources available to the researcher. There are three main sampling strategies: purposive, quota and snowball.

Purposive sampling

Purposive sampling is the most common strategy open to qualitative researchers and occurs when participants are grouped according to pre-set criteria relevant to the research study, for example pregnant mothers who smoke during their pregnancies, or infertile women undergoing fertility treatments. In some research studies, it is important to the research question to ensure that the participants in the research exhibit the characteristics the researchers wish to investigate. In other studies there are no essential criteria, as the research question is broad rather than specific – for example students on undergraduate nursing programmes. The more specific the research question, the more specific the criteria for inclusion and exclusion from the study. In purposive sampling, the number of participants may be determined by resources available to the researcher, or the point at which theoretical saturation occurs. By this, we mean the point in data collection where new data no longer bring additional insights to the research question.

Quota sampling

Quota sampling is a type of purposive sampling. However, the size and characteristics are determined prior to data collection at the stage of study design. Characteristics might include students studying a particular programme, in a particular year of study, or of a particular age, gender or ethnicity. Setting criteria in this way allows the qualitative researcher to choose participants who are most likely to have an insight into the focus of the study. The researcher determines the criteria, then goes into the community or population of interest and collects data from that group until the quota is reached. Purposive and quota sampling depend on the identification of participants based on selected criteria.

Snowball sampling

Snowball sampling is also a type of purposive sampling. However, this strategy depends on respondents identifying individuals known to them who might be interested in participating in the research. Snowball sampling is particularly useful with hard-to-reach groups. However, it does depend on identifying initial respondents who then 'get the snowball rolling'. When using snowball sampling the researcher needs to be mindful of the problem of bias, in that the technique itself reduces the likelihood that the sample will represent a good cross-section of the population.

It is worth noting that in qualitative work the researcher is not rigidly bound by the original sampling strategy. It is acceptable to mix sampling strategies or to refine the strategy depending on the progress of data collection. This flexibility allows sampling for later stages of the research to be guided by earlier findings.

Collecting qualitative data

Direct observation

In qualitative research, where it is important that the researcher is immersed in the area to be studied, data are collected through observing people in their own environments. This might be the observation of a particular occupational group, such as nurses, doctors or physiotherapists, or observations of patients in healthcare settings. The aim is for the researcher to develop an understanding of the values and beliefs held by the population under investigation.

Participant observation

In direct observation information can be collected by a *participant* observer. For example, a nurse undertaking normal duties may observe the processes going on in a care setting and collect data during the course of a shift. Alternatively, a *non-participant* observer, for example a non-nurse, may observe nurses at work and collect data during the course of a shift. Both approaches are legitimate and the choice depends on the research question. Take for example a research study where the aim is to understand the interpersonal relationships between nurse managers and ward staff over the course of a working day. Here it would be difficult for a researcher who is not part of the nursing team to have complete access to the full range of activities that make up the nursing 'work', for example day-to-day care, team meetings, ward rounds and handovers. It is unlikely that a non-participant observer would come to understand how interpersonal relationships between members of the nursing team play out in the day-to-day life of the ward. On the other hand, a participant observer, for example a member of the nursing team, would naturally participate in a range of nursing activities where interpersonal relationships are a key feature of the working day. Thus the observer would be able to collect the data required to answer the research question in a way that enhances the trustworthiness of the findings.

Participant observation in qualitative research is viewed on a continuum, whereby at the extreme the observer is completely immersed in the area under investigation. In this case, the observer is usually a natural participant and may be observing a situation of which they are naturally a part. At the other end of the continuum the researcher may be quite external to the observation, in some cases observing through the medium of television, video conferencing or other media. In most cases participant observation falls somewhere in between. James Key (1997) identifies five types of participant observation, namely external, passive, balanced, active and total, all of which allow for more or less interaction with the participants. However, each type relies on systematically seeking out and organising data, the concern being with what is studied rather than focusing on achieving a situationally defined goal. The participant observer keeps detailed records of everything that occurs, including those things normally taken for granted, or naturally occurring in the setting. In addition, the participant observer periodically removes him- or herself from the situation in order to review data collected from a neutral position and monitors observations constantly, recording data in an unbiased way.

Non-participant observation

In non-participant observation, the researcher watches the subjects of the study with their consent, but takes no active part in the situation. A key consideration here is that most people, on knowing they are being observed, will usually act differently to some degree, a phenomenon known as the 'Hawthorn effect', a termed coined to describe the behaviour-modifying effects of being the subject of social investigation, rather than the context of the investigation. One way in which researchers can mitigate the Hawthorn Effect is to observe similar situations over time, although this has obvious resource implications. Alternatively, video recording equipment is used, although this only limits the Hawthorn Effect and does not eradicate it.

Interviews

Interviews allow for the collection of detailed data from the population studied, which can be analysed in detail later. Interviews can take place in any setting, and are usually located at a place convenient to respondents and researchers, i.e. a mutually agreed time and location. Quantitative data collection techniques such as questionnaires may include open-ended questions and facilitate data collection from large numbers of respondents in a way not permitted by interviews. However, the potential of the interview to permit probing of issues of interest to the researcher that may pre-exist the interview or which occur as the interview proceeds remains one of the key benefits. Interviews can be in-depth, structured, semi-structured, informal or formal.

In-depth interviews

In-depth interviews are usually conducted at a venue convenient to the respondent or mutually agreed by respondent and researcher. The key to successful interviewing is for the respondent to feel at ease and for the researcher to be well prepared before the interview begins, which may require equipment for audio recording the interview, and an interview schedule, either structured or semi-structured. This necessitates forward planning in order that time is used effectively and data collected are meaningful and appropriate for the study. In-depth interviews allow the researcher to gather data rich in depth and detail. Unlike a survey used in quantitative research, the researcher rarely has a pre-determined set of questions, as the objective of in-depth interviewing is to encourage the respondent to express their views at length in their own words. As we saw in the previous chapter, qualitative research requires the researcher to allow the participants to guide, control and direct the inquiry. Therefore the skill of the in-depth interviewer is in facilitation, rather than controlling the process of data collection.

In-depth interviewing leads to particular challenges for the researcher, not least in ensuring that the data collected are appropriate to the study. For this reason, the researcher may choose a structured or semi-structured approach.

Structured interviews

A structured approach to interviewing is appropriate when the interviewer is familiar with the subject matter of the research. Although not a survey as such, a formalised questionnaire can be used to direct the interview along a pre-determined set of questions. The respondent is able to answer the questions in their own words. However, the degree of flexibility is far less than in semi-structured interviews. The main advantage of structured interviews is their ability to allow sequencing of questions, which subsequently facilitates sequenced analysis. This approach would not lend itself to those qualitative methodologies in which it is imperative to give complete freedom to the respondent, for example in narrative research. However, when using grounded theory inter-viewers may use a progressive focusing technique, whereby the researcher asks the respondents a pre-determined set of questions which have arisen from prior data collection. Although answered in the respondent's own words, this focused or structured approach allows the researcher to pursue ideas and questions grounded in the data (Holloway, 1997). A further reason for choosing a structured approach is when the researcher wishes to undertake a large number of interviews but prefers not to undertake a survey, which generally lends itself to quantitative research. In this case, a structured approach may enable the more effective use of resources with the interview guided in terms of questions and available time by the use of a structured interview guide.

Semi-structured interviews

Semi-structured interviews use an open framework. The key is to facilitate a focused two-way conversation between researcher and respondent. The usual method in this approach is to start the interview with a general question and move to specific questions as the interview progresses. The specific questions may or may not arise out of the previous questions, i.e. as a response to answers given earlier. A semi-structured approach is useful, in much the same way as a structured approach when the emphasis is on making the best use of available time and effective use of resources, such as availability of respondent, researcher and facilities for conducting the interview.

A semi-structured approach allows consideration of relevant topics prior to the interview. A greater degree of flexibility than with a structured approach allows the opportunity for deviation from the prescribed topic. In semi-structured interviewing, while the topic is identified beforehand, the majority of questions are created during the interview itself. An interview guide used in semi-structured interviewing is for framing the interview and not for directing it *per se*.

Focus groups

Focus groups are a form of group interviewing with a subtle difference, in that the key feature of the focus group is the interaction that takes place between the respondents. Unlike group interviews, in which the researcher may interview a number of respondents at the same time with the emphasis on questions and responses between researcher and recipients, the focus group relies on interaction within the group prompted by topics supplied by the researcher (Morgan, 1997). The reason for choosing focus groups to collect qualitative data, rather than other methods such as one-to-one interviews, group interviews or questionnaire surveys, lies in the ability of the focus group to draw out the attitudes, feelings and beliefs that individuals may hold on a given issue through the process of social interaction. The emotional processes and multiplicity of views elicited through group interaction are a powerful tool for the qualitative researcher. However, the very nature of the focus group and its capacity to draw on respondents' core attitudes, values and beliefs requires a skilled interviewer and thoughtful preparation before undertaking this method of data collection.

Focus group interviewing requires the researcher to have an interview 'guide prior to beginning the focus group. It is important for the researcher to ensure that the focus group achieves its aim, which is to enable all participants to discuss and comment on the issue fully while avoiding the tendency for any one participant to take over and dominate proceedings to the detriment of other voices. In this sense, an individual interview may be easier to control than a focus group in which participants may take control. A well thought out interview guide enables the researcher to draw participants back to the topic at hand and to remain in control of the process should the topic move too far from the focus of the research. Focus groups can be extremely useful for exploring dynamics between groups, where the researcher is interested in power relationships between decision-makers and professionals, or where everyday use of language and culture of particular groups is of interest (Morgan, 1997).

Focus groups are particularly useful in a participatory action research context, in that they provide an opportunity for participants to be involved in the decision-making process, to be valued as experts, and to be given the chance to work collaboratively with researchers – all key features of participatory action research. In this sense, focus groups can be extremely empowering. However, the researcher choosing to use the focus group technique needs to be mindful that some participants may be less articulate, less confident, and often more introvert than others. In these situations some participants may find the focus group intimidating and consequently not as empowering an experience as for other members of the group. From a practical point of view, focus groups need time to set up. Efforts need to be taken to ensure a representative sample within the group, which may be difficult if respondents feel themselves to be inarticulate, lacking in confidence, or have communication difficulties. If this is the case then rather than compromise the research and alienate respondents who may have an important contribution to make other methods such as individual interviews should be considered. The final point to make about focus groups (and individual interviews for that matter) is that they can never be completely confidential or anonymous, as information is shared with the group. Participants in the focus group should be made aware of this before consenting to take part. The researcher, for their part, should set ground rules for all participants in the focus group to address the ethical issue of confidentiality. Although information is shared within the group and will be used for the purposes of the research, participants must be encouraged not to share information outside the group. The researcher must anonymise all data collected from the group to ensure that no individual participant can be identified.

Documentary sources

In some cases it is not possible to gather data from participants: a particular group may be inaccessible, no longer viable or in existence; may be unwilling to participate; or may have been overused in research. In certain situations, to subject groups or individuals to further research would be traumatic, for example victims of crime, abuse or extreme trauma. In these situations it may be possible to collect data or supplement existing data with documentary evidence.

A number of different sources are available as documentary evidence, and these can be central or peripheral to the study. Documentary evidence may derive from private or public material, for example minutes of private meetings, legal documents or confidential reports, or documents in the public domain such as textbooks, academic journals, and other archived materials. A distinction is drawn between the formal or informal nature of documentary sources; for example, diaries, journals and memoirs may constitute informal sources, as opposed to more formal documents such as official reports. 'Documentary' is sometimes applied to data collected from oral narratives and certain non-textual objects such as works of art (Simms and Wright, 2000). Documentary sources used retrospectively are generally considered as secondary research, in that the data were created or assembled before the current research was carried out. Data not specifically created for the research is deemed a secondary source on which primary research is being carried out. As such, primary data are always subject to primary analysis, whereas secondary data may be subject to either primary or secondary analysis.

A criticism of the aforementioned qualitative methods of data collection, and indeed of qualitative research in general, is that only small numbers of participants can be studied because data collection methods are so labour-intensive. In addition, qualitative research is often criticised for being subject to researcher bias, difficulties in analysing qualitative data rigorously, and the lack of reproducibility and generalisability of the findings. We consider strategies for overcoming these difficulties next.

Qualitative data analysis

Qualitative data analysis is the process where we proceed from data collection to interpretation, explanation and understanding of the participants and situations of interest to us. In keeping with the philosophy underpinning qualitative research, where we are interested to know what a given situation or experience was like for the individual, the idea is to come to know someone's view of the world: how he or she came to that view, and what meaning they attribute to their experience. For the majority of data collection in qualitative research, be it from interviews, focus groups, case study or role-play, the process of data analysis involves the key steps of coding and identifying themes (Lewins *et al.*, 2005). In discourse analysis or other forms of narrative research, identification of themes may not be required. Seidal (1998) likens qualitative data analysis to a jigsaw puzzle and uses the framework of noticing, collecting and thinking to structure the analysis of qualitative data.

Noticing

Noticing things in the data may initially begin with making observations, writing field notes, audio recording interviews and gathering documents, the point of which is to produce a record of the things we have noticed. Once the record is produced and subsequently focused on, further interesting things may be noticed in the data. As these interesting things are noticed, they are coded. Coding in the manner described here allows the data to be collected together. The researcher searches the collected data for types, words, sentences, phrases, patterns or wholes, with the aim of reconstructing the data into a meaningful or comprehensible account. Codes are used to pull together and categorise what would otherwise be confusing and unrelated accounts.

Collecting

Lewins *et al.* (2005) begin their guidelines on qualitative data analysis by considering what it means to write about the data collected. They suggest that what the researcher initially writes may contain some analytic ideas; in other words, the process of analysis begins early. On the other hand, the researcher may simply summarise data, with the analytic process coming later. Whatever the approach, the point of writing is to organise the data into manageable parts in order that the identification of themes can begin. Coding the data is an essential part of this process.

Coding allows the application of labels to sections of the data that look as though they might belong to a theme. For example, in qualitative research undertaken with South Asian student nurses, collected from face-to-face interviews, we were interested to know of their experiences of studying an undergraduate nursing programme (Dyson *et al.*, 2008). The researchers read the interview transcripts and circled what seemed to be key words, phrases or events, writing short notes at the side of the circled text. This initial coding led to a list, part of which we show here:

- negotiation with family to leave home to study at university
- nursing as a positive career choice
- fear of failure
- perceptions of support from tutors at university
- career aspirations

As you can see, some parts of the list are simple descriptions of what the students said (for example, fear of failure), whereas other parts are more analytical (for example, nursing as a positive career choice). This list (abridged here) was used to 'mark up' the rest of the transcript and other transcripts in order that comparisons could be made. Negotiation to study recurred across the transcripts and generated the theme: negotiated journeys.

Thinking

Once the process of collecting and sorting has been undertaken, the next step in qualitative data analysis is to think about the data. In the thinking stage the researcher is engaged in examining the collected account, the goal being to make sense out of what has been collected together, to look for patterns and relationships within and across collections and to make discoveries about the phenomena being studied.

There are, of course, some criticisms of the model of qualitative data analysis presented here, namely, the process of breaking down the data into small parts can destroy the totality of the philosophy as expressed by the interviewee. The very act of breaking down the data into its constituent parts can sometimes distort the analysis. A way round this is to work between two accounts or transcripts; a coded version and an intact version. In this way, the researcher can work back and forth between the parts and the whole. There are alternative ways of analysing qualitative data that do not involve the process of noticing (making notes and writing about the data), collecting (coding the data) and thinking (looking for patterns, identifying themes within and across the data). The model of noticing, collecting and thinking does run the risk of describing the codes but losing the phenomena. Nevertheless, it is an extremely useful and pragmatic approach to qualitative data analysis.

Computer-based qualitative data analysis

Qualitative research can produce large amounts of data in the form of interview or focus group transcripts, often running to many pages. With the advent of computer software packages, Qualitative data analysis can be managed efficiently without losing the quality of the analysis. Computer-assisted qualitative data analysis allows not only the coding and retrieval of text, but also for rapid searching through the transcripts that would ordinarily take the researcher an age to do – hence the cost-effectiveness of using computer-assisted qualitative data analysis. However, should this technology be used, the researcher must invest the time and effort to ensure they are familiar with the program. Integral to this is an understanding of what the software can and cannot do. In general, computer-assisted qualitative data analysis, whichever package is used, provides the researcher with a workspace in which to work through information quickly and easily. Tools within the package assist in classifying, sorting and arranging data, which would otherwise be managed by hand. This frees up time for exploring trends, finding meaning and arriving at answers. The computer assists the researcher with data management but does not *think* for the researcher.

Conclusion

We have considered strategies for identifying respondents in qualitative research including purposive, quota and snowball techniques. We noted that qualitative researchers might draw on a mixture of approaches or refine the approach as data collection proceeds in order to achieve theoretical saturation. We then looked at techniques for collecting qualitative data, including observation, interviews, and focus groups. These techniques rely on the presence, to a greater or lesser extent, of participants in the research. We also considered analysis of texts and documents, a method available to qualitative researchers when collection of data from individuals is difficult or impossible. There are other methods of collecting qualitative data: for example diary methods, where the researcher or participant keeps a personal account of daily events, feelings, discussions and interactions; role play, where participants play a role or observe role play prior to rating behaviour; and case study, which is an in-depth study of one person, group or event.

Finally, we looked at qualitative data analysis, focusing in particular on Seidal's (1998) model of noticing, collecting and thinking. Within this model, we have looked at coding the data prior to identifying and organising into themes. Seidal's model allows more detailed approaches to qualitative data analysis to be carried out within its broad framework, including the constant comparative method and the extremely detailed method of qualitative data analysis used in grounded theory and described in the pervious chapter. Criticisms and inherent risks of Seidal's approach to qualitative data analysis are noted, in particular that coding involves breaking the transcripts down into small parts with the result that the integrity of the expressed account may be lost. One solution to this problem is to working back and forth between a coded account and an intact account. Finally, we considered the benefits and disadvantages afforded to qualitative data analysis in using computer-assisted packages. In the next chapter, we consider quality and ethics in qualitative research.

Further reading

Silverman, D. (2009) *Doing Qualitative Research*, 3rd edn. Sage, Berkshire.

Holloway, I. (ed.) (2005) *Qualitative Research in Health Care*. Open University Press, Berkshire.

Pope, C. and Mays, N. (eds.) (2006) *Qualitative Research in Health Care*, 3rd edn. Blackwell, Oxford.

CHAPTER 4

Qualitative research: quality and ethics

Introduction

So far in this book we have looked at research philosophies, methodologies, methods, data collection and analysis. We have learnt that qualitative research is concerned in the main with the systematic collection, ordering, description, and interpretation of textual data generated from talk, observation or documentation. Qualitative research methods of data collection are many and varied, including interviewing, observation and documentary analysis. Whatever the method, the aim of qualitative research is, as Kitto *et al.* (2008) suggest, to explore the behaviour, processes of interaction, meaning, values and experiences of purposefully sampled individuals and groups in their natural context. Quantitative research, on the other hand, is concerned with the size or extent of a phenomenon. Data are collected and subjected to statistical tests, to allow prediction and generalisation to the broader population.

Given the difference in frameworks for data collection and analysis in qualitative and quantitative research, it is fair to suggest that considerations of quality be approached differently. The conventional criteria of validity, reliability and generalisability as applied to quantitative research do not fit with qualitative research, for reasons that the goal or aim is intrinsically different, as are sampling strategies, including sample size. Consequently, the criteria of clarification and justification, procedural rigour, representativeness, interpretation, reflexivity and evaluative rigour, and transferability are used to ensure a comprehensive framework for addressing quality in qualitative research (Kitto *et al.*, 2008).

Clarification and justification

In an earlier chapter we looked at research methodologies used in qualitative research, focusing in particular on ethnography, phenomenology, grounded theory, action research, narrative research and feminist research. In all these forms of research, clarity of purpose and how this is translated into the research aims and objectives is essential to addressing concerns of quality in qualitative research. The qualitative researcher must pay attention to, and be able to demonstrate, a rigorous approach to determining the best fit between the research question, aims and objectives, and the chosen methodology and methods of data collection. For example, if the aims of a research project are to understand from the perspectives of the respondents what it is like to live with a long-term condition, then an appropriate methodology may be phenomenology, given that phenomenology assists participants to reveal dimensions of the lived world, so that the lived world is revealed . Alternatively, if a researcher wishes to understand cultural practice in a busy accident and emergency department, and how nurses experience working in this multidisciplinary setting, then ethnography would provide a best fit, as it allows the researcher to study respondents in their everyday context. This is not to say that only one approach or design will suffice to the exclusion of all others. As discussed earlier, methodological blindness, where the researcher claims to have found the one true methodological position, limits the potential for qualitative research to enable respondents to tell their stories in their own words. Rather, the question is one of clarification and justification on the part of the researcher as to why a particular approach as opposed to an alternative. Thus, clarification (what is the research question) and justification (why this approach to the research design) are integral considerations for the qualitative researcher.

Procedural rigour

Procedural rigour in qualitative research refers to the transparency adopted by the researchers in reporting and recording each step in the research process. Each step should be open to scrutiny and should hold up under rigorous questioning. For example, it should be clear how respondents were identified and approached, how consent was obtained to involve respondents in the research, where and how data were collected, and how data were recorded, transcribed and stored. These are legitimate questions for the research audience and if left unanswered may raise doubts as to the quality of the research. On the other hand, with a transparent approach to reporting the procedures for data collection, readers and recipients of the research can be confident in the quality of the research findings. The level of detail in the account of how data were accessed and handled may be limited in qualitative research, depending on the inclusion criteria of different publications and the requirements of different research audiences. However, qualitative researchers (indeed all researchers) must be able to show, upon request, how research findings were arrived at. Intellectual property rights and ethical issues of confidentiality afford protection to the researcher and respondents and are addressed later in this chapter. However, the important point here is to ensure that data collection techniques and approaches to data analysis are completely transparent.

Representativeness

Representativeness in qualitative research refers to the measures taken for ensuring the sample of respondents in the research study represents the population of interest to the researcher. In a previous chapter, we learnt that the number of respondents in qualitative research might be relatively small as the aim is not to generalise to the broader population, but rather to understand from the perspective of the individual what it is like to experience a given phenomenon. In similar conditions, it may be possible to transfer the findings of a particular qualitative study to other settings. However, this is not the overall aim of qualitative research, which is to give a voice to the individual, rather than to predict for whole populations. What is important from a quality perspective is to be clear as to how the respondents in the research were identified. A number of approaches to sampling in qualitative research are available and the researcher needs to make clear which was used. For example, qualitative researchers may take a homogeneous approach to data collection with respondents selected in relation to specific criteria. Sample size may be limited by the availability of respondents who fit the given criteria, or by the data collection method (interviews, focus groups) or available resources. Snowball sampling is an alternative technique often used when respondents are difficult to identify. This approach allows each respondent to identify another respondent until the researcher is satisfied that the research question has been addressed or no new data are forthcoming. An alternative method of qualitative data collection is convenience sampling, whereby the respondents are readily accessible to the researcher. Whatever the approach to data collection, the researcher must be able to justify the method in relation to issues of bias. In this sense, the latter approach is most open to question and the qualitative researcher should exhaust other forms of sampling before resorting to using a convenience technique. Most importantly, the qualitative researcher should be transparent regarding the technique used and able to justify why it, rather than any other, was employed. Alternative approaches should be considered and a rationale provided as to why these were not appropriate in a given research study. The important consideration for the qualitative researcher is whether the chosen sampling technique facilitates transferability or conceptual generalisability. By this, we mean, whether or not the audience can be confident that given similar situations the research findings have generated significant enough insight into the phenomenon under consideration to allow transferability to other settings.

Interpretative rigour

Interpretative rigour refers to how qualitative researchers deal with and present the data. To minimise the risk of bias within the analysis, qualitative researchers often use the notion of inter-rater reliability. This involves a process of triangulation where more than one researcher is involved in the data analysis process. In this way, the validity and reliability of qualitative data is enhanced. Transcripts are coded and themes identified by each member of the research team before being shared across the team. This process of sharing and discussion allows for a more nuanced approach to data analysis. A related technique is that of respondent validation or member checking, whereby the actual respondents in the research are given the opportunity to read and review the transcripts from their interviews. Respondent validation, if undertaken, is best performed as close in time to the actual data collection as possible, as recollection and/or interpretation of events may decrease over time.

Techniques for enhancing interpretative rigour include different methods of triangulation, for example using a variety of documentary sources, multiple methods of data collection, or more than one theoretical framework for data analysis.

Reflexivity

Consideration should be paid by qualitative researchers to the relationship of researcher to respondents. The nature of qualitative research in health and social care often finds the researcher known to the respondents and familiar, if not to the respondents themselves, then with the research setting. Were this not the case, important research into aspects of health and illness would remain the remit of independent researchers with little or no insight into issues of relevance to those individuals most affected by the phenomenon under consideration, namely the patients and those involved in their care. However, measures need to be taken by qualitative researchers to ensure that the quality of research in situations where researcher and respondents may be known to each other is not compromised. Reflexivity is where open acknowledgement is made of the relationship between researcher, research topic and respondents. Qualitative researchers must be able to demonstrate how their value systems impact on the research question, design, data collection and data analysis.

Transferability

We have previously referred to transferability in qualitative research as a more appropriate concept than generalisability, given the aim of qualitative research: to understand from the individual's perspective what it is like to experience a particular phenomenon, and not to makes predictions for whole populations. In terms of the quality of qualitative research, transferability or conceptual generalisability refers to how well the research findings may usefully inform health care settings other than the one in which the original research was undertaken. Qualitative researchers need to be mindful of claims made about their research findings and avoid overplaying or overstating the case. In order for qualitative researchers to be confident in the transferability and applicability of their research to similar health care settings, attention should be paid to the following:

- clarification and justification of the research question
- transparency in detailing the steps in the research process
- representativeness of the sampling strategy
- careful interpretation of the findings with useful employment of triangulation
- consideration of the relationship between researcher, respondent and the context of the research

Ethical issues in qualitative research

Ethical approval is required for all research undertaken within the health and social care field, to protect the respondents and to ensure the maintenance of ethical standards. The National Research Ethics Service (NRES) exists to facilitate ethical research that is of potential benefit to participants, science and society, and provides an ethical review of proposed research via its Research Ethics Committees (RECS). The purpose of the REC is to ensure consideration of the rights, dignity and well-being of research participants by the researcher(s) and it is on this basis that the REC makes its decision to approve the research, to require amendments to the research proposal or indeed to reject the proposed research. The Social Care Research Ethics Committee is part of the NRES and has a remit to review adult social care research proposals. Universities and other organisations typically require ethical approval for research carried out by their employees, or on their behalf, including student research, and will facilitate ethical approval through their own research ethics committees.

Research in health and social care is carried out to contribute to the health and well-being of those who take part in it. When thinking about ethical issues in research a polarisation of research into quantitative and qualitative is not helpful, as ethical issues cut across the philosophical divide. Having said that, the qualitative methods considered in this chapter, for example ethnography, phenomenology, action research and narrative methods, do pose certain ethical challenges for the researcher. We now look at these in detail.

Informed and voluntary consent

Potential participants in research must be fully informed about the nature of the research, the demands it may make on them in terms of time and resources, and the potential benefits or indeed risks associated with participation before they make a decision to take part. Informed consent not only requires that adequate information is given to participants, but also that participants are capable of comprehending the information and have the power of free choice to voluntarily participate or to decline, without actual or perceived coercion. In this sense, informed consent is a two-step process with information about the research provided first, usually in an information sheet, followed by written consent, using a consent form.

In qualitative research data collection usually requires participants to consent to be interviewed either face-to-face, or by telephone. Interviews can be lengthy and may have the potential to cause anxiety for the respondents. It is essential that participants are aware of exactly what they are consenting to, including where the data collection process will take place, what will happen to the data once collected, how it will be stored and for how long. Participants should be informed that they have the right to withdraw from the study at any time should they wish to do so and to know what will happen to any data collected from them, up to and including the point of withdrawal. Participants should be provided with details of how to complain about the conduct of the research or researchers without having to ask for this information.

Confidentiality and anonymity of research participants

Participants in research have the right to expect that information collected from them is kept in strictest confidence. Anonymity occurs when the researcher cannot link a participant with the data collected from that participant, for example, when a questionnaire is used to collect data and it is returned to the researcher with no identifying details on it. However, as we have seen, qualitative research involves the collection of data from individuals in their own words, usually through interviews or focus groups. In these situations the researcher makes a promise of confidentiality to the respondent and guarantees that any information will not be publicly reported or made accessible to anyone other than the research team, unless explicit consent has been obtained to do so from the participants. Consent should be obtained from participants for agreement to use direct quotations, which is often a feature of reporting qualitative data. When directly quoting respondents verbatim, i.e. word for word, the respondent is anonymised or assigned an identification number or letter. In focus groups, where a number of participants are brought together, agreement should be sought at the beginning, from all involved, to respect the right to privacy.

Doing no harm, doing good and reciprocity

In qualitative research the potential to cause physical harm to participants does not arise in the same way as it might in scientific research, for example in clinical trials of new treatments. However, it is entirely possible for psychological harm to occur during qualitative research, especially when using in-depth data collection techniques. The qualitative researcher must be mindful of this and, although not necessarily refraining from asking probing questions, must do so with sensitivity. In the event that respondents become distressed, the researcher should be prepared in advance and should have access to support for the participants and for themselves should this become necessary.

Conclusion

In this chapter we have looked at issues of quality in qualitative research. We focused in particular on the criteria of clarification and justification, procedural rigour, representativeness, interpretation, reflexivity and evaluative rigour, and transferability, using Kitto *et al.*'s (2008) framework for addressing quality in qualitative research. We have shown that ethical issues in research are as important a consideration for the qualitative researcher as for the quantitative researcher. Ethical considerations are integral to all steps in the research process from initial research question, through to research design, data collection and analysis, presentation and dissemination of results. Paying attention to ethical issues in qualitative research is key to assuring the quality of the research in terms of its rigour, dependability and reliability.

CHAPTER 5

Quantitative research: experiments

Quantitative methods are based on the scientific method. Science has a huge impact on our lives, and a vast amount of funding is poured into it all over the world. The scientific method clearly has a lot going for it, but what can it contribute to our research? Nurses have choices when it comes to using research methods. The next two chapters will explore some of the options that quantitative research can offer. It will also point out some of the limitations.

Experience of teaching nurses about quantitative research methods has shown that, on the whole, most nurses are rather reluctant to learn about this topic. If you had to, which of these blank boxes would you tick?

	Strongly disagree	Disagree	Neutral	Agree	Strongly Agree
I understand a lot about quantitative research					

At the simplest level, quantitative research deals with numbers. For some people this is a real problem. However, if you are a qualified nurse, then by definition you must have at least a basic understanding of mathematics – which puts you in a strong position. If you can work out a warfarin dose or load a syringe driver with morphine, you can definitely do quantitative research. On a personal note, I only *just* passed my mathematics Scottish Ordinary Grade examination (many years ago), but I now teach quantitative data analysis to university students. Something must have changed over the years, and it is not that I became more intelligent! Other people have discovered this too. Field (2009) has produced probably the most detailed book on statistics currently available for non-statisticians and he also, in the introduction, describes how he 'turned on' to quantitative data methods late in the day, due to an excellent teacher.

Fortunately for all healthcare workers interested in quantitative methods, the days of researchers having to deal with complex formulae, usually involving Greek letters and undertaking vast calculations are now over; we have computers to do this for us. If you have the computing skills to do your monthly budget on a Microsoft Excel worksheet, you can analyse data, present your findings and publish. There are a number of computer programs available; this book will at times refer to SPSS (formerly 'Statistical Package for the Social Sciences'), which is globally one of the most widely used statistical programs.

Which statistical packages are available to you?

Here is an early exercise for you to undertake:

1. Find out which statistical package(s) are in use within your Trust, or if you are studying, within your university.
2. Find someone who can show you what it is capable of, and ask for a demonstration.
3. Think about the sort of research findings you could analyse using such a package.

A note of caution is necessary here; although statistical packages make this analytical power available to the researcher, some of the concepts are still quite challenging. It is up to the reader to decide whether it is worth the investment. Another warning – it can be addictive!

What are the quantities in quantitative research?

Quantitative methods deal in numbers. They measure the quantity, or amount, of a phenomenon. With numbers we can give clear answers to questions, for example:

- Does antipsychotic drug A result in better client outcomes than B?
- How satisfied are clients with the outreach service?
- Do students understand quantitative data analysis lectures?

This makes quantitative methods very powerful. It is easy to imagine that, when considering investing millions of pounds on an intervention, some hard nosed questions will be asked. Take the first example above. Trust managers have a lot of responsibility and big budgets. Drug A is a new antipsychotic which is cheap. The board would like to use drug A for acute in-patients, but is concerned that if it is not as effective as the current 'gold standard' (i.e. the best drug conventionally used), drug B. Using drug A could reduce the drug budget, but also result in patients who had uncontrolled symptoms. Their recovery may take longer and there may be unpleasant side effects resulting in longer stays over a six monthly period, all bad outcomes for both patients and Trust. The drug may be cheaper, but not cost-effective.

If we are qualitative researchers, we could investigate the *quality* of their experience. We might:

■ get valuable narratives regarding their stays
■ identify what was important to the clients in terms of services and care
■ possibly get a feel for how debilitating side effects were

What we cannot do is *quantify* it, i.e. measure *how much* better (or worse) the new drug is.

By comparison, if we are quantitative researchers, we can use established reliable and valid assessment scales to actually measure whether the clients in group A were better or worse off than group B *and by how much*: the differences can be quantified, or measured.

We can also pull in other data such as:

■ lengths of stay
■ how many patients did not tolerate the treatment
■ how many developed serious side effects

We can use quantitative data analysis to present the Trust board with a report of these findings. If you were on the board, which methods would you rely upon to make your judgement?

Main types of quantitative research

Bowling (2009) classifies quantitative research into two main groups, experimental and non-experimental. This structure will be used here. In practice, this produces two main types of exploration: the classic experiment and the survey. This is not an exhaustive classification, but it does cover the majority of the quantitative research which is published and is largely relevant to nursing and health care.

Hypotheses and research questions

The first step in designing a quantitative research project is to clarify what is to be researched. The traditional method is to set a hypothesis. A hypothesis is a statement of the researcher's expectations about the relationship between two variables. A variable is any item which can vary and be measured, for example body weight (measured in kilograms) or exercise tolerance (measured in number of metres run). Note that both of these variables can be mathematically represented.

The hypothesis is therefore a prediction which links the two, for example: 'an increase in body weight will reduce the level of exercise tolerance'. This can then be used as a basis to construct an experiment.

Exercise

Identify an issue within your clinical area which could be worth exploring using an experiment. Identify the two variables involved and formulate an initial hypothesis. Having done this, build in more detail. One very clear way to do this is to state who is being experimented upon. Using the example in the paragraph above, if it is formulated by a nurse working in a cardiac rehabilitation clinic, then the client group should be included:

'an increase in body weight of patients following myocardial infarction will reduce the level of exercise tolerance'.

The more detail the better; a well formulated hypothesis will guide the experimental design.

Null hypotheses

Traditional scientific development is built upon taking a body of knowledge, making deductions and then testing them. It is only when parts of this body of knowledge have been shown to be wrong that real scientific progress can be shown to be made. Therefore, although it seems rather complicated, in experimental research using quantitative data analysis it is more usual to form a *null hypothesis* (Parahoo, 2006), for example, 'an increase in body weight of patients following myocardial infarction will *not* reduce the level of exercise tolerance'. Null hypotheses may be scientifically desirable but can be confusing. For this reason it is quite acceptable to stay with a standard hypothesis, particularly if it gives clear guidance as to what is being researched.

Exercise

Take your hypothesis identified above and convert it into a null hypothesis. Does this clarify the issues for you?

Experimental research

Experimental research is derived directly from the scientific method. It is based upon two main components:

- Researchers introduce an intervention or treatment
- A measurement is made of the effect (if any) of the treatment

If in your research question you have statements comparing one treatment with another, or exploring the effects of an intervention (e.g. education, new techniques in wound dressing or working practices), then experimental research is likely to be the way forward.

Here is an example of a very badly designed experiment, which meets these criteria. Read through it and spend 10 minutes answering the questions:

Turbo D Experiment

I am interested in whether the fruit drink I give my children causes them to become more hyperactive than usual, so I decide to set up an experiment.

I invite a dozen of their friends round. Half of them get new 'Turbo D', an E number- and caffeine-enriched drink; half of them get pure spring water.

They all drink 250 ml of their drink and then play for one hour.

At the end of the hour I assess their behaviour.

This qualifies as an experiment, just, but is it likely to give me accurate findings?

- How likely is this to give me an accurate idea of the effects of 'Turbo D'?
- What factors are likely to get in the way of me getting accurate findings?
- How would you improve it?

Analysis

It is possible that, if carried out, this experiment might get some interesting findings, but it seems unlikely that they would be either reliable or valid. Clearly it is definitely not acceptable to carry out unannounced experiments on small children, but there are also a number of items which must be clarified.

The first one is the variables concerned. A variable is something which can be measured. Nurses commonly are involved in identifying variables in their practice:

- dosages of drugs
- amount of fluid input
- amount of fluid output

Others include age, gender, shoe size etc. In quantitative research we are interested in defining the variables, because this will ensure that we are very clear as to what we are measuring.

In the Turbo D experiment above, to say 'at the end of the hour I assess their behaviour', is of no value. What variables are we going to measure? Because this is quantitative research they need to be quantities which we can assign a number to. For example, I could:

- Hire a radar gun and measure the speed which the children run past me (miles per hour)
- Count the number of times they run into each other (number of collisions per minute)
- Measure the volume of noise in my garden using a sound pressure meter (decibels)

All three could be measured at the same time, perhaps to pick up on different aspects of their behaviour. Therefore if the variables can be defined, we can start to be clear as to exactly what we are measuring, and hence determine the effect of the drink.

The next item is the *sample* of children. Twelve is a very small number to include in any experiment and causes a problem. I may already have a number of hyperactive children in the group, because one of my children is himself hyperactive. Whatever happens to the group, it is likely that these children will produce atypical findings: they will introduce *bias*. This means that the group will not behave as a more representative group of 'normal' children would. Finally, consent is a major issue for nurses. Clearly it is not acceptable to experiment in a haphazard way with children, who constitute a vulnerable group. In experiments in healthcare, people themselves are experimented upon, their treatments are changed and they may be exposed to hazard. Experimental research therefore requires stringent ethical consideration. For those interested, a useful starting point is the National Research Ethics Service (NRES) homepage (NRES, 2008).

The Turbo D experiment, for all its faults, however, does contain the basic structure of an experiment.

Constructing an experiment: some terminology

Quantitative research has its own terminology and it is worth becoming familiar with it. The special characteristic of an experiment which sets it apart from all other types of design is the ability to show *cause* and *effect*. This means that if you wish to introduce a new treatment, then setting up an experiment will give you the evidence to show that your treatment either works or does not work, meaning that if the treatment is introduced (cause) it will have a predictable outcome (effect) on a *population*.

The population is the group of people whose behaviour you wish to be able to explore or predict. In the Turbo D example, the group might be children between the ages of 10 and 12 living in England. Clearly it would be impossible to experiment with this whole population, so a *sample* is chosen, the maximum size commonly being limited by the resources available to the researcher. If the sample is chosen carefully then it should be possible to transfer or generalise the findings to the larger population.

The treatment which is manipulated is termed the *independent variable*, e.g. the administration of Turbo D in the previous example. This is compared with a control treatment. In the health care setting this is usually described as a 'gold standard' conventional treatment. This means that if the patient is not included in the experimental group, they can be assured that they will get the best conventional treatment, as decided by existing evidence.

The *dependent variable* is what you measure. In the Turbo D example, this was not specified, but some options have been outlined, above. One or more of these variables could be chosen.

Here is an example from healthcare science. Thomas *et al.* (2009) set up an experiment to compare two non-pharmacological methods for treating clients with asthma in primary care. One hundred and eighty three asthma clients were randomised into two groups. This means that each client had the same chance of being in one or the other group. This again reduces the likelihood of bias. The comparison was between two groups: those who received physiotherapist-supervised breathing training (the independent variable) and nurse-delivered asthma education (the control group). The dependent variables were numerous, but one of the main items was the Asthma Quality of Life Questionnaire (AQLQ), which has been shown in other studies to be sensitive to the well-being of asthma patients. The experiment showed that at one month there were similar scores between the two groups, but at six months the breathing training resulted in more favourable scores. This experiment shows a clear cause and effect, and it can be concluded that if breathing specialists are in a position to provide one of the two treatments, there is a strong case to use breathing training.

Controlling the experiment

As shown in this example, in a healthcare setting, the independent and control variables can be complex. Imagine you are a patient undergoing major surgery and are approached by a researcher exploring pain control. You might, initially at least, be interested in helping with their research. Most patients are well disposed to help promote care. However, if the choice was that one half of the patients received a new promising drug for pain control (independent variable), or a placebo, i.e. have no effective pain relief (control variable), then only the very brave or very foolish would take part.

In healthcare then, the most common contrast, is between the experimental treatment (dependent variable), and what can be described as a 'Gold Standard Conventional Treatment' (control variable). This is also a part of the ethical process. NHS Trust ethical committees, NRES and clinicians themselves have a duty to safeguard the participants of experiments. They insist, therefore, that at worst the participants will have a good standard of treatment: one which is research- and evidence-based, and is thoroughly up to date. This will then be compared with the experimental treatment, which has been shown in preliminary trials (also termed phase I and II trials; to be discussed later), to be likely to be at least as good as, and possibly better than, the Gold Standard.

Therefore, taking the example of the surgical patient already mentioned, the independent variable is the new drug and it would be compared with an agreed standard intervention which has been shown to deliver good quality pain relief, a patient-controlled opioid system for example.

Dependent variable

This is what is measured. The experiment is designed so that changes due to the manipulation of independent variables are picked up by the dependent variable, either immediately or later. For example, changes in pain using the surgical experiment outlined above could be assessed in a number of ways:

- Patients are asked to use a visual analogue scale every hour on which they score their pain on a scale from 0–10.
- Heart rate and blood pressure are recorded (the basis here is physiological: that pain would cause an increase in both).
- Patients are given a questionnaire on discharge, asking them how well they felt their pain was controlled.

Clearly a lot of expertise is required to pick sensitive and relevant dependent variables, and this is at the heart of good experimental design. To help with this it is worth taking time and scholarship to develop a detailed research question or hypothesis.

Exercise

Figure 5.1 shows the basic structure of an experiment which has been annotated to show the variables in the Turbo D example. Using the hypothesis you produced earlier in the chapter, take five minutes to draw your own version. Identify and include the independent and dependent variables. Give as much detail as you can, including for example, the length of time between manipulating the independent variable and measuring the dependent one.

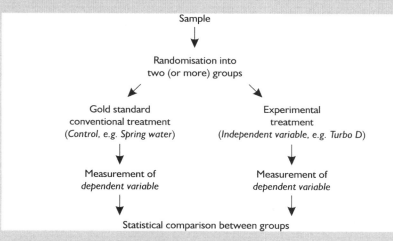

Figure 5.1 Basics of experimental design.

Sampling in quantitative research

The basic principles of sampling in quantitative research are quite straightforward. The researcher wishes to measure the impact of their treatment within a population. If resources such as time, money, administrative staff etc. were available, the entire population would be included in the research. This is seldom possible, so a smaller representative sample is selected. Whenever a sample is chosen, there is the opportunity to introduce sampling error, which can produce *bias* (Sapsford, 2007). Bias means a deviation from the true value of the population, and is due to a wide range of variability within people. By definition, not everyone can be included within a sample. Results in this situation are likely to be skewed, i.e. pushed away from more representative values. As anyone knows who has worked in health care, people come in a wide variety of sizes, shapes and responses to even the most straightforward suggestions. If a sample of 10 subjects is used within a research project, it can be conjectured that one or two extreme cases will produce unrepresentative or biased results. If the sample is then increased to 100 or 1,000 subjects, the unrepresentative subjects are likely to become progressively diluted. Therefore in quantitative research in general the larger the sample size, the better (Shields and Twycross, 2008).

How large should a sample be?

Power analysis is the branch of statistics which shows the size of sample that is required to distinguish an effect in, for example, an experimental setting. It is not intended in this book to explore power analysis, but there are some basic rules. Firstly, the larger the difference in the dependent variable between groups (*effect size*), the easier it is to detect. Secondly, some statistical techniques are more able to distinguish between groups (they are described as being *more powerful*). Lastly, it depends on how much the researcher wishes to expose themselves to error; if they are very stringent, then again a larger size is required.

There are two types of error. Type one error is where it appears that there is a difference between groups, but in fact it is not real (also known as false positive error). Type two error is where it appears as though there is not a difference between two groups, but in fact there is (also known as false negative error) (Greasley, 2008). As can be seen, this is quite complex and whole books have been written about power analysis. For a good summary which is easy to read, try page 12 of Anthony (1999).

Another way to avoid too much theory is to use a statistical package to predict sample size. One excellent example of this is G*Power, which also has the advantage of being free. At the time of writing (mid-2010) it can be downloaded from http://www.psycho.uni-duesseldorf.de/abteilungen/aap/gpower3/.

Sample size: some rules of thumb

Running some examples through G*power does allow us to make some broad predictions, which might be useful if the student wishes to make a research proposal. These examples are based upon using a *t* test to detect differences between two groups. This is one of the standard tests used within experiments and is quite powerful. G*power uses Cohen's widely used criteria for weak, medium and strong effects, and for the technically minded type one error was set at 0.05 and type two error at 0.8 (these are standard criteria as outlined in Anthony (1999)).

- If an experiment has 40 participants, split into two groups, it is only likely to be able to detect a strong difference between groups.
- If an experiment has 90 participants, split into two groups, it is likely to be able to detect a medium or large strength difference between groups.
- If an experiment has 500 participants, split into two groups, it is likely to be able to detect a weak, medium or large strength difference between groups.

From this discussion it can be seen that if we are interested in effects which have real clinical significance, i.e. are at least of medium effect, then a sample size of greater than 90 will be likely to produce findings which may have impact in the real word, i.e. identify at least medium effects. To summarise, the message is quite clear, in quantitative research a large sample size will support the ability to pick up differences between groups, and the larger the better!

Sampling strategies

There is more to sampling in quantitative research than just getting the largest feasible number of subjects, however. It is important to have a clear sampling strategy, so that the group identified in the research question is represented fully in the research itself, otherwise the research will not be valid.

Probability sampling

In probability sampling, a formal attempt is made to represent the population within the sample. It can also be described as a strategy in which each member of the population has an equal chance of being selected. There are many sampling strategies in print, and often different terms are used to describe similar strategies and vice versa. What follows is a reasonably simple category of sampling strategies which from reading health care research describes perhaps 95% of the published literature. It is based upon principles found in Bowling (2009) and Polit and Beck (2008).

Random sampling

This is the most straightforward way to undertake probability sampling. A random sample is taken from the population up to a pre-determined maximum number. *Random* means to have no specific pattern, purpose or objective. In more scientific terms and applied to sampling, it means that each person within the group has the same likelihood of being chosen. This means that subjects or events are chosen with no pattern at all between them. The classic example of this is to make a list of names of subjects, cut the list up, fold them over and put them in a hat (or other receptacle). The names are then taken out one by one until the sample is complete. Each name has the same chance as any other to be included within the sample. This is such a powerful technique that it has actually escaped from research terminology and become part of everyday English, we may talk about 'taking a name out of the hat' to suggest some sort of sampling in common situations. This works well for small projects, but more sophisticated methods have been developed using computer-generated randomised tables.

Randomisation is the classic 'scientific' sampling, but relies on large samples to represent the population. It has already been suggested that, within an experiment, subjects are randomised into the two (or more) treatment groups. This is seen as being of great significance in the evidence-based practice movement, supporters of which would argue that without true randomised sampling, it is impossible for an experiment to illustrate cause and effect.

Stratified sampling

A stratified sample is one which the individual has an equal chance of being chosen in relation to their proportion within the total population. This is particularly valuable within the health care setting, where different groups of individuals have different needs and expectations. Nurses in the UK, for example, are currently differentiated in work and payment by their pay bands. When undertaking research with a group of nurses, it might be felt necessary to include a proportion from each band to get the full picture of the workforce. This is particularly useful in survey research. Strictly, there should be a proportionate selection from each group (stratum means a layer; hence stratified) as shown in Table 5.1.

Table 5.1

Agenda for Change Banding	5	6	7
Total number of staff	300	100	50
Number include in sample	60	20	10

In this example, a 20% sample has been taken from each pay band within the population, so that the researcher can be confident that the proportion of subjects from each pay band is the same in the sample as it is in the wider population. Sampling can then take place within the strata, ideally using randomisation. One point to note here is that if a large randomised sample was taken, then by definition the different groups would, if the sample were large enough, all be proportionately presented. Stratified sampling is therefore very useful in the situation where a smaller sample only can be used.

Inclusive sampling

An inclusive sample is where everyone within the population is included. This is in many ways the ideal, as it removes the possibility of bias within the sample, by definition. However, it depends on the size of a population as to whether this is possible. It is a very attractive sampling strategy within some heath care settings, when relatively small populations are sampled. For example, if undertaking research regarding hand washing by nurses within a hospital ward, there might only be 30–40 nurses to sample from. The simplest strategy is then to include the whole population within the research. The limiting factor becomes the researcher's resources and ability to deal with the full population. Nursing research is often placed within a ward, or community setting, and in this type of setting inclusive sampling may be easily achieved. Note that if an inclusive sample is used, bias is avoided because the whole population, by definition, is used; the sample *is* the population.

Non-probability sampling

It may not be possible to include a sufficiently large number of examples to represent the full population, or to gain access to the full population. If this is the case, then a non-probability sampling technique may be necessary. This means that there is no sustained effort to represent the entire population. Instead, the researcher effectively samples as many subjects as he or she can, using the resources available to them. These techniques largely *do not* use a random sample and some bias will probably be involved. Therefore, if used with an experimental design these techniques introduce limitations which should be addressed within the research team and discussed when writing the experiment up. If resources are limited (which is usually the case), although less than ideal these techniques may still allow robust research to take place.

Purposive sampling

This is a branch of non-probability sampling. The researcher identifies the quality which makes the sample group relevant to the researcher. For example, an educationalist might wish to sample students from years one, two and three of a nursing programme. A sample of the students are then accessed and invited to take part. It is the 'hand picked' nature of the subjects which distinguishes purposive (sometimes called purposeful) sampling; it means that although the subjects will all be directly relevant to the research (an advantage), the sample is specialised and probably biased and may not be applicable to the wider population (a disadvantage). Again, for experimental research this means that the ability to justify cause and effect becomes limited, but it does not mean that the research becomes invalid. It means rather that the findings have to be applied with care, and the limitation of the sampling should be acknowledged.

Convenience sampling

This is the weakest form of sampling to be discussed here. Literally it means that the selection of subjects suits the convenience of the researcher, e.g. the researcher chooses the first five subjects to come through the door, or similar method of access. Typically this is as a result of having limited resources, but as discussed above, although it is a limitation to the quality of the research, it does not make good quality research impossible. It does, however, move further way from linking cause to effect and produces more caution in applying findings to practice. Using the example of the nursing students above, if the first 50 students to enter the coffee room on campus are chosen, the sample is likely to be biased – they may make an unrepresentative proportion of caffeine-depleted, and hence possibly depressed, subjects, and quite possibly should be avoided.

Similarly, within practice, if the first five patients on a morning list for minor surgery are sampled there is likely to be bias; the consultant may have arranged for the more straightforward cases to be dealt with first.

Randomised controlled trials (RCTs)

In some ways RCTs represent the most formal scientific approach to research. RCTs are very highly specified experiments. They are important because if a company wishes to launch a new drug or medical procedure onto the market, there are very high standards to be met to ensure that it is (a) safe, (b) likely to be better than currently existing drugs and (c) cost-effective. To do this, RCTs are used in healthcare, education and other fields. These provide evidence to statutory bodies. In the UK, for example, if there is any concern that a treatment may not be effective or may be prohibitively expensive, the National Institute for Clinical Excellence (NICE) will investigate to determine whether or not the treatments represent best practice and best care. A similar role is undertaken in the USA by the United States Food and Drug Administration.

There are classically four phases in an RCT (adapted from Polit and Beck, 2008).

■ **Phase I**: Safety, feasibility, acceptability
The inventors of the new treatment feel that they have a promising product and start to explore its properties. Moving from animal trials to humans, they explore useful doses, safety and possible side effects. At the end of the Phase I trials, the researchers will have an idea of who the drug may be effective for and how to use it. Typically this takes place outside of the NHS and is run by private companies and clinics.

■ **Phase II**: Preliminary effect size, side effects, dosing
Evidence is built up exploring the effectiveness of the treatment. Phase II uses small trials and commonly some quasi-experimental designs to build up a picture of the possible clinical use of the product. This phase can be described as a pilot or exploratory stage.

■ **Phase III**: Efficacy of new treatment compared to standard
This is the full experimental test of the treatment. Typically it takes place (in UK healthcare) within NHS settings. It is a full experiment, and contains a number of elements. As a piece of high-quality experimental research, a large

sample size is necessary. This may include hundreds or even thousands of subjects. The control group is supplied by using a 'Gold Standard' conventional treatment. This must be based upon the latest available evidence in order to gain ethical approval for the trial. As the name suggests, randomisation of the sample is important. The split between the control and experimental group is provided by a randomised process, so that participants have an equal chance of being in either group. To obtain a large sample size, RCTs are commonly spread over a number of sites, and may be termed 'multi-centre'. To minimise the introduction of bias, groups are commonly 'blinded', an unfortunate term which means that they are unaware which treatment is being used. With single blinding, the subject is not aware of whether they are in the experimental or control group. With double blinding, neither patient nor clinical staff are aware of which treatment is used for a particular patient.

The Hawthorne effect

Blinding is designed to minimise the 'Hawthorne effect'. The Hawthorne Works was a factory near Chicago USA which produced all the switches for American telephones – it was a big factory. In the mid-1920s its working practices were explored by researchers. It was found that whenever the researchers were present, productivity increased. In research terms, an unacknowledged independent variable was the knowledge that the workers were being studied. Similar effects can be suggested which are relevant to healthcare. For example, if it is known that staff are being observed as they wash their hands, then it is likely that during the study, staff will take more time to wash their hands, and be more particular as they do it. Once the study is over, staff become more relaxed and probably will move back to their previous habits.

■ **Phase IV**: Application in clinical setting; long-term safety

Once the treatment has been adopted and is in practice, this is not the end of the story. The long-term effectiveness of the medication is researched plus the occurrence of side effects. In time, new interventions and drugs will be produced and further comparisons will be made through experimental and other forms of research.

Impact of RCTs

RCTs contribute directly to clinical decision making. They are described as being high-quality evidence (Grey, 2009). Here is an example. There is a condition called essential thrombocythaemia, where the bone marrow produces too many platelets. As a result, people with this condition are at risk of thromboses and, if the count is very high, of bleeding. An RCT was undertaken, called the PT-1 Trial, taking subjects from New Zealand, the UK, Australia and France. It compared two drug treatments: hydroxycarbamide plus low dose aspirin and anagrelide plus low dose aspirin. So strong were the findings that hydroxycarbamide plus aspirin was the better treatment (at least for high-risk patients) that the trial was halted, and this is the recommendation used widely in the UK (Harrison *et al.*, 2005). This information has been made widely available to the public through educational materials, such as those produced by Leukaemia Research (Campbell, 2006).

Should I take part in RCTs?

This is inevitably a personal choice. Occasionally subjects taking part in trials are featured in the news. For example, in 2006 a Phase I trial of an anti inflammatory drug TGN1412 was started in the UK. This left six volunteers seriously ill and two, at one point, possibly close to death. Fortunately, all eventually survived. However, by their nature Phase I and II trials have an element of risk, and this is why subjects are paid to take part – in the case of TGN1412, it was reported that volunteers were paid £2,000 each (Rosenbaum, 2006).

There is a much stronger case to be made for taking part in Phase III trials. By this stage, manufacturers will already have a good understanding of the drug (for example). More significantly, they will have managed to convince a formal ethical committee that their drug is likely to be at least as good as conventional treatments, and there is a likelihood that it may actually be better. So, if taking part and receiving the test drug, a positive case can be made for a good outcome. However, this is also the case if given the control, because part of the research design is an assurance that all non-experimental group subjects will be given up-to-date evidence-based findings. Therefore if given an opportunity to take part in a Phase III trial, there is some evidence that it is likely to be of benefit to the subject in either arm of the trial. This is one case of philanthropy also being of self-benefit.

Conclusion

Experiments remain a mainstay of scientific enquiry. If correctly set up and conducted, they can identify cause and effect, which no other form of research can. Their scientific pedigree is both their strength and weakness. They can show the connection between variables, but because of this they may have limited use amongst nurses. Nursing, by definition, deals with delivering care to clients. Clients are almost infinitely complex and may be better served by non-deductive methods, such as qualitative research, to investigate their worlds. Similarly, it may not be possible to construct experiments on complex issues which involve degrees of patient choice. If this is the case, a survey may be one form of quantitative research which can be more flexible in investigation.

CHAPTER 6

Quantitative research: surveys

Surveys are possibly the most commonly undertaken form of research. They are so popular that they have 'escaped' into everyday usage. Most readers will, at some time, have completed a survey, perhaps in the high street, or by post from their bank, to provide marketplace information.

Surveys are rightly popular because they are extremely flexible and can be constructed and modified to answer a wide variety of research questions. They are very good at showing *association*, but not causality. For example, a survey could be undertaken of nursing students asking them about their use of cannabis and their mood state. There is a lot of interest currently in this topic, and it has been suggested that recent forms of high-strength cannabis, such as 'skunk' may precipitate mental health changes. It might be found that students who smoke cannabis indeed have a lower mood state than those who do not, but this does not prove that the cannabis caused this. It might instead be suggested that students with a low mood state are likely to seek out cannabis for relief. Therefore the association between the two may be shown, but not proof that one causes the other. If cause and effect is required, then an experimental structure is required. This, however, is probably impossible. No ethical committee would agree to a research project where large groups of nursing students were given cannabis and were told to smoke it! In this sort of situation, a survey may be the only suitable research design which is available.

Within an experiment a survey-style questionnaire may be included (commonly referred to as a data collection tool); so there is some common ground between the two. However, surveys should not be seen as a poor relation to experimental work. They can provide valuable information, and if well constructed may answer the research question in good detail.

Research questions for nurses

As has been discussed, nursing research embraces both quantitative and qualitative methods. The use of a hypothesis, null or otherwise, is necessary for a traditional scientific way of exploring issues and so works well for experiments. In nursing research it is more common to use a research question. There are a number of reasons for this. Certainly in inductive, qualitative work, we cannot really identify the variables we will be working with. Instead, the work is commonly designed to find what the variables are, rather than test them. The enquiry is therefore more tentative; there is no pre-existing model of which variables will affect the results. One way to address this is to use a looser structure to start the enquiry, and this is often posed as a research question (Polit and Beck, 2008).

When deriving a research question, it is still possible to include variables which have been identified as being worthy of exploration. Here is a hypothesis used in the previous chapter:

Increase in body weight will reduce the level of exercise tolerance.

By comparison a more open-ended *research question* could be:

How does increase in body weight affect the way people exercise?

When phrased this way, the question is more open and less predictive. This allows a more creative process of research. The answer is not going to be 'yes' or 'no'.

Using research questions in higher degrees

This approach can be particularly useful if you want to include qualitative elements of study, a common strategy with higher degrees. PhD studies collect findings over a period of three years (full time) or five years (part time). Within this time frame they may have two, three or even more phases of their project (Holloway and Walker, 2000; Phillips and Pugh, 2005). Commonly, the first step of the research is to find out which variables are the important ones in a particular setting.

Here is an example from a real-life PhD, exploring how the use of a computerised data management system would affect nurses working within critical care. Even if pressed to do so, it would not have been possible to state a hypothesis, because it was not clear at the outset what the variables were. Instead, to guide the study an open-ended research question was posed ('What are the factors which affect the way nurses use a computerised data management system?'), and this gave guidance to the first qualitative phase, which used interviews to identify the main issues. It was then possible to set up a comparative quantitative exploration to identify which of these variables were important, in a similar way to setting up an experiment.

In summary, therefore, the use of a research question works well for mixed method designs, where a hypothesis would be too limiting. It also works well for surveys.

Exercise: Setting a research question

A clear and simple research question is a good start to a research project using a survey.

Most research questions have two main items:

- Who is going to be researched?
- What is the focus of the research?

Take a look around your clinical area and identify an aspect of practice which you think could be improved. Draft your research question as one simple question, for example:

- How do critical care nurses assess mouth care in ventilated patients?

In this case it is clear who is being researched; it is the nurses working within critical care. There is also clarity regarding the focus of the work, including specific details of the group of patients they care for.

This is quite different from formulating a hypothesis. It is more open ended, it predicts less and it gives freedom to choose a range of research tactics. This question could be explored using a survey.

Look at the research question you have drafted; is it clear who will be researched and is it clear what the main focus will be? If you are looking for the relationship between two variables, then an experiment may be the best way to proceed, if the question is open-ended, then a survey may be the best way to proceed.

What is a survey?

Surveys have a long history. Sapsford (2007) identifies that the 11th century Domesday Book is one of the earliest surveys, listing all the manors and farms of England for the purpose of taxation. This meaning of surveying survives as a term used in geography and architecture; before buying a house, we have it surveyed to find its value and identify any architectural problems.

The sort of survey to be discussed here is more specialised. Although qualitative surveys are feasible, this chapter will focus on the more common quantitative research surveys, using systematic methods to gather specific information from a specific population. To do this, it is wise to start with a clear research question, which can be used to construct a suitable questionnaire, which will produce reliable and valid findings (Bowling and Ibrahim, 2005).

Types of survey

With a direct survey, the researcher typically approaches a sample of the target group and may interview them or ask them to fill in a questionnaire.

With an indirect survey, written oral and visual records can be surveyed. Data may be entered in a data collection tool, so again production of a clear, structured questionnaire is at the centre of a well-conducted survey. There are a number of ways to conduct a survey, but the classic form of survey is the quantitative questionnaire sent or handed to an individual, with clear instructions as to how to complete and return it to the researcher. This will form the basis of this chapter.

Surveys can be carried out at one point in time, and these are termed *cross-sectional*, in that the survey is given out across an entire sample. Cross-sectional surveys are typically *descriptive*, in that they literally describe the phenomenon of choice, for example the incidence of falls in the elderly, or the incidence of side effects caused by a drug. In addition to these target data, surveys usually contain demographic data which describe the population, for example age, gender, rank or pay band. This information can be very useful as it allows the researcher to explore the characteristics of the different groups within the sample, which can add depth and meaning to the analysis (this will be discussed in the quantitative data analysis chapter). Surveys can also be retrospective, looking back on activities perhaps by reviewing a selection of patient notes in a doctor's surgery.

With a cross-sectional survey, a snapshot is gained of the activities being surveyed. Survey work can be extended over a period of time, the questionnaire being given out at different time intervals; this then becomes a *longitudinal survey*, which follows the progress of a population. An example could be a questionnaire exploring morale within an organisation, which is given out every year, so that changes in staff attitudes can be identified over a period of time. This may also be termed an *analytic survey* in that it analyses changes which take place, and will involve statistical analysis to identify how the population has changed and whether this is statistically significant.

What can be surveyed?

The short answer is almost anything can. Surveys are extremely flexible. If a questionnaire item can be framed which goes some way to answering the research question, then a survey can be conducted. With more items within the questionnaire, a fuller picture of the population response can be developed. As questions accumulate, the survey questionnaire begins to take shape. An issue to consider is the provenance of these items within the questionnaire. For a questionnaire to be valid, the source of the items should be clear. They may be generated from qualitative research such as focus groups or interviews, from background reading or from other sources. This seems obvious, but a questionnaire which can prove its provenance is likely to be robust and to produce valid findings, rather than one in which the questions are thought up by the researcher in isolation. By illustration, a small abstract painting on canvas may be attractive and fetch £50 or even £100, but if it is anonymous it is unlikely to be very valuable. With seven letters in the lower right-hand corner it may be worth millions, particularly if they spell 'Picasso'. In addition, Fink (1995) suggests that an expert could be used to review items and Gillham (2000a) identifies that piloting is an important step to support this process.

Non-healthcare surveys can be used for political and consumer choices. Researchers can use surveys to explore feelings, motivations, plans, beliefs and perusal background (Bowling, 2005). Translated to health care, issues can include satisfaction with services, how services can be improved, wellbeing and health status, lifestyles and exposure to disease risk factors. With a survey, the questionnaire is the central component. It may be necessary to invest time and energy in making it easy to read, easy to use and likely to produce valid results, but once this has been done it is essentially as easy to give to 10, 100 or even 1,000 respondents. This is a very attractive proposition for researchers and goes some way to explaining the popularity of surveys.

Who can be surveyed?

In the previous chapter, it was identified that experiments largely required probability sampling to make them robust. Probability sampling is also suitable for surveys, and is generally recommended, in line with 'scientific' processes. However, surveys do not rely on their sampling in the same way, as they do not claim to identify cause and effect; because association is less stringent than cause and effect (i.e. it makes fewer claims). Other strategies are available and justifiable, and may be classified as non-probability sampling. These have been discussed in the previous chapter.

Response rates

Surveys are not like experiments. There is no way to control the variables, even in a longitudinal survey. One issue which exemplifies this lack of control is response rate. A survey can be drafted, piloted and administered. Part of the ethical considerations involved in health care research is the issue of consent. A common way of addressing this is to assume that completion and return of the questionnaire is evidence of consent to take part. This means that it is unethical to force or pressurise participants to complete the survey. Commonly this means that response rates are low or at best variable and this can introduce bias.

All surveyors would hope for a high response rate; for example, greater than 90% would be excellent. This is seldom achieved though. A response rate greater than 70% is often considered adequate. Experience has shown that amongst nurses and other healthcare professionals 50% is an achievable target, and amongst student nurses it may be somewhat lower (for an example see Norrie and Dalby, 2007). Exactly why this should be the case is not always clear. Within a health setting, nurses and other workers are commonly very busy and may be pressurised to complete their work on time, so filling in yet another questionnaire may be a very low priority. Similarly, paperwork in healthcare settings may itself be a burden for workers. There may be an issue of 'questionnaire fatigue'. Finally, staff may be suspicious of the questionnaire, and see it possibly as a management tool. What results therefore is a bias in the return sample, which may be severe. However, this does not mean that a survey should be abandoned because, for example, it only achieved a return rate of 35%; it does, however, mean that the low return rate should be discussed and acknowledged, and if it is wished to utilise such a survey's findings in practice it would be wise to seek support from other research literature. Emotive topics such as domestic violence and sexual content may generate lower returns, and an unsolicited survey, where there is not prior contact with the subjects, may have a response rate less than 20%.

To overcome this tendency for a low response rate, researchers have a number of tactics. One is to offer inducements to respond. This could include entering names into a lottery draw of some sort, but this may compromise anonymity. Another is to offer a small token of thanks, and for those working with nurses it may come as no surprise that these tokens are often in the form of chocolate!

One more formal tactic which should always be used is a clear explanation of the aims of the research, including an outline of what the nurses, or clients or service might gain from the work. This should be part of a Participant Information Sheet which accompanies the questionnaire. These, however, should be couched in broad terms, or they may influence the ways in which the questionnaires are completed.

Bearing this in mind, it is still important to have an approximate guide to the size of sample to be aimed for. Teddlie and Tashakkori (2009) use the data in Table 6.1 to show the relationship between sample and population sizes.

Table 6.1 Sample size and confidence.

Population size	Confident that the sample estimates population within plus or minus 1%	Confident that the sample estimates population within plus or minus 5%
100	99	80
500	476	218
1,000	906	278
2,000	1,656	323
3,000	2,286	341
Infinity	9,604	384

Clearly, the larger the sample size, the more confident we can be that the sample represents the population. Indeed, this table illustrates that with small populations it is necessary to sample the majority of the population so as to be confident that the data are representative. However, as the population increases, if we use the plus or minus 5% category, which is a level of confidence that most survey researchers would think acceptable, there is a plateau effect; samples in the range of 300–400 appear to be broadly representative of their populations. If the sample size increases above these values, then the researchers reduce the amount of variance from the true population, but the extent to which this is achieved then becomes a matter of resources.

Two caveats are necessary, however. Firstly, this table is predicated upon using a probability sampling technique. Therefore it holds with inclusive sampling, but if non-probability sampling, such as a purposive strategy, is used the statistics should be approached with caution. Secondly, it does not address response rates. If a target of 350 responses is the goal, then a generous margin should be incorporated to optimise the chances of getting this total, for example by distributing at least 700, assuming a 50% return rate. Furthermore, in data analysis of surveys it is often desirable to explore differences between groups using inferential statistics, so there may be a need for power analysis, as discussed in Chapter 5.

How to construct a quantitative survey

Surveys commonly start with a section of demographic data. This section gives information about who is completing the survey. Items can include age, gender, ethnicity, clinical band, qualifications and how long respondents have been in post or within the speciality. These serve to summarise the population, but they also are useful in the application of inferential statistics, where one group is compared with another to see if there is a real difference in experience. For example if exploring violence and aggression in a clinical area, it seems likely that women and men will have different experiences, or that exposure to these may be influenced by ethnicity.

There are a number of choices available of items within the survey proper. As this is a discussion of quantitative research methods, qualitative items will not be explored, although there is a role for these too (see later).

In quantitative surveys, the data produced will at some point be coded and entered into a database. This may be a familiar program such as Microsoft Excel, or a dedicated statistical package such as SPSS (formerly Statistical Package for the Social Sciences). SPSS is probably on a worldwide basis the most commonly used package in universities. One strategy is to enter data directly into Excel, which is widely available on computers running Microsoft Windows, and when all the data are prepared they are cut and pasted into SPSS.

In a quantitative survey most items are closed questions or statements. This means that there are a limited number of responses. These responses are allocated a number during coding, and the numbers entered into the database.

Here is an example from a piece of research looking at exposure to violence and aggression.

How often have you felt uncomfortable/threatened/unsafe due to aggression in your workplace?

❑ Never
❑ Seldom
❑ Occasionally
❑ Regularly
❑ Most days

The responses are coded from one to five, so if the box 'Occasionally' has been ticked, then a 'three' is recorded. If the box 'Never' has been ticked, a 'one' is given. For data such as these which contain a scale, it is common to make coding intuitive; this means that as the likelihood of being threatened increases, so does the score given to it. Coding therefore funnels the information so that a questionnaire is summarised by a string of numbers, which can then be statistically analysed.

There a number of different levels of data which can be included in a questionnaire. In general, the higher the level of data which can be used the better, as it provides more information and can allow more detailed analyses to be carried out (Anthony, 1999). One final note: *data* is a plural; the singular is *datum*.

Nominal or categorical data

These are the lowest forms of data. With nominal data there is no ordering to the information. They typically provide yes or no responses. Examples include:

- Are you pregnant?
- Do you have a previous history of hypertension?
- Were you provided with medications on discharge?

Here is another example:

Is your pain:

- ❏ Flickering
- ❏ Throbbing
- ❏ Tingling
- ❏ Crushing

There are choices here, but there is no order to the information. My pain may be tingling, but that does not mean it is more or less uncomfortable than a crushing or flickering pain. Another obvious example is gender; people on the whole are male or female. However, even here there may be some contention. If the study were to be set in a gender reassignment clinic this might need some re-working as a questionnaire item. In this circumstance it may be better to use a more sensitive way of measuring to what extent a client feels male or female, perhaps on a scale from 0–10. This then produces data with an order to them, termed ordinal data.

Ordinal data

With ordinal data, there is an order but not a fixed relationship between points. A good example of ordinal data is the numbering of motorway junctions.

Between London and Leicester there are 21 junctions on the M1 (ignoring newer junctions such as 15a). When map reading, these can be ticked off and it is straightforward to identify that there are 3, 6, or 10 junctions to go, which is very useful for navigation. However, the distance between motorway junctions can vary widely, from one to two miles (junctions 2–3) to more than 10 miles (junctions 20–21). The order is fixed, but the distance between points varies. Another example is swimmers finishing in a race. Giving the order (first, second, third) gives important information, but does not tell by how much the race was won. Ordinal data are very widespread in healthcare research, particularly in quantitative surveys. Two common types are described below.

Likert scales

These were first developed by a North American social researcher, Rensis Likert (pronounced Lick-urt) in the 1930s. Most people will be familiar with a Likert scale questionnaire, as they are widely used in marketing and research, and have been for the last 80 years.

A statement is made, and the respondent is invited to tick a pre-formatted statement which corresponds with their level of agreement. One issue of note here is that although included within a questionnaire, Likert items are not actually questions! A range of options are possible; perhaps the most common is the five interval scale:

(1) Strongly disagree (2) Disagree (3) Neutral (4) Agree (5) Strongly Agree

There are variants of this, a common one being a four-item scale where the neutral category is omitted, forcing respondents to choose between being positive or negative in response. Oppenheim (1992) gives a very detailed discussion of the options available in the design and usage of Likert scales.

Visual analogue scales (VAS)

These are probably familiar to most health workers who assess client reactions. Respondents are asked to place a mark on a visual scale to represent experiences such as pain, or wellbeing.

Example: My pain is:

0	5	10
Nil		Severe

The data are again ordinal, and can be analysed in exactly the same way as Likert scales

Being creative

One very useful aspect of using scales is that it may not require words at all. Here is an example (Figure 6.1) used by David Dalby of De Montfort University, exploring the satisfaction of clients with a Learning Disability with their service. It has some of the characteristics of a Likert item and some of a VAS.

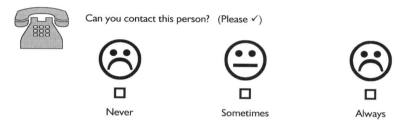

Figure 6.1

How clients use it will vary, as does the extent of disability, but one way would be to read the question out to the client, and ask them to identify which of the 'faces' they would identify with. Similar methods have been use in pain assessment for pre-reading children. This ability to be creative is very attractive and can lead to new and exciting methods (Grbich, 2004).

Interval level data

With interval level data, the distance between items on the scale is constant. A car travelling at 30 mph is definitely travelling at half the speed of a car at 60 mph. Interval level data are used less frequently in research which explores beliefs and subjective responses. Thus if a questionnaire is being constructed to explore patient satisfaction, then it may be that only some minor items such as demographic data, particularly age, length of service etc., may be interval data. However, there are important uses for interval level data, especially (but not only) in medical research:

- Length of time survival following myocardial infarction
- Optimal dosages of drug for medical conditions
- Age at which a diagnosis is made
- Patient's oral temperature following administration of paracetamol

The attraction of interval data is that they are cited as being a prerequisite for a number of important statistical techniques which include the tests which classically analyse the outcomes of experiments, and many other techniques which are used in statistical modelling. However, these techniques are robust, and there are a number of researchers who successfully apply these statistical analyses to larger sets of ordinal data as long as they meet certain criteria, which will be discussed in the next chapter.

Developing a questionnaire using ordinal data

Here is an example of a Likert scale item, which the reader has already met:

	Strongly disagree	Disagree	Neutral	Agree	Strongly Agree
I understand a lot about quantitative research					

Which box would you now tick? Hopefully, some of the readers will have increased their scores since the start of these chapters (perhaps not).

Trying to sum up a response to quite a complex topic such as the world of quantitative research with a single-item questionnaire would be unwise. As may have been discovered, there are lots of different topics within quantitative research methods. Some are actually quite straightforward, others definitely not so. How could one question encompass the lot?

Here is another example. If I were to invite a number of friends to my house for their evening meal, as a quantitative researcher (there is after all no such thing as a free lunch) I might produce a questionnaire to see how much they enjoyed it. I have a number of options:

- *Using nominal data* I am quite limited: did you enjoy the meal? The responses could be only yes or no, which provides me with limited information.
- *Using ordinal data* is better: I could make a statement 'The meal was excellent' and put it in a Likert scale format (Strongly disagree – Strongly

agree). This would be better, but it ignores the fact that a good meal is made up of a number items, some of which may have been good, others awful.

Use of a single score is too crude. It cannot tell if there are different factors to be explored. In addition, one poorly constructed question may ruin the survey entirely.

It would be more sensitive to identify a number of items which might describe the experience of the meal, for example, the size of the portions, the quality of the wines which accompanied it, how well seasoned it was etc. This results in a bank of Likert items, all of which relate to the meal. Taken overall, each item contributes to the assessment of the quality of the meal, and each contributes its own unique quality.

Here is an example of part of a questionnaire (there were originally 12 items, which have been edited down) used in a research project to explore the ways in which critical care nurses record patient data (adapted from Norrie and Dalby (2007)).

Part A: Identify and categorise the different components used
Which year of your studies are you in:

Year 1 ☐
Year 2 ☐
Year 3 ☐

1) Which branch are you in?
Mental Health ☐
Learning Disability ☐
Child ☐
Adult ☐

2) Are you undertaking a
Degree ☐
Diploma ☐

Part B: For each item, please tick one box only which best describes your opinion

	Strongly agree	Agree	Disagree	Strongly disagree
It is important to me to know which subjects I need to learn				

I prefer to manage my own learning				
I seldom add to my learning with independent study				
I like to be thoroughly prepared before starting a module				
I like to be taught rather than finding out on my own				
I do not find exploring the experiences of others is a good way of learning				
I like to know why it is important to learn a topic				

Part C: In your own words, can you briefly identify the best methods which help you learn?

Discussion: The first item is a set of demographic questions, identifying the year of studies, nursing branch and programme. This allows us to summarise who the population are, specifically who has completed the questionnaire. These data can also be used to see if there are differences in response according to any of these criteria, to compare groups. Techniques for doing this will be discussed in the next chapter. The second item is a bank of Likert scale items, which all explore different aspects of ways in which the student nurses learn, based upon focus group work. If all the items score consistently high or low, then the questionnaire is said to be internally reliable, which is a hallmark of good quality.

Alpha analysis

Quality is assessed by using a statistical test called an alpha analysis (Field 2009). The highest possible alpha score is 1.0. This would mean that each item gave essentially identical responses, meaning that the questionnaire was asking the same question (in this case) seven times. If the alpha value is low (for example 0.2), then the questions are identifying a number of different issues within the responses. In this case, individual items would be investigated and reported.

With a moderately high alpha (greater than 0.7–0.8) it is usually safe to summate the scale. This means that the responses for each item can be added up and an overall average score take. This then represents the body of the questionnaire, and is much more dependable than asking one question. Including qualitative elements in a survey

Finally, although this is overwhelmingly a quantitative questionnaire, there is still a place for some qualitative work. Coming from a deductive methodology produces a possible weakness. The questionnaire was produced following a focus groups with nurse lecturers to identify the issues which they felt were important. However, this is not to say that *all* the important issues were included. Therefore it is a common strategy of quantitative researchers to include a small number of open-ended questions in order to identify inductively any items which may have been missed from the questionnaire which are of importance to the respondents.

Ways to improve a survey

The survey should always be piloted before use. To draw up a questionnaire is fairly easy. However, the researcher may be oblivious to a number of faults within it. Although to him or her it may seem clear and unambiguous, the author is always biased, having created it and possibly lost objective perspective on it. These may threaten its validity. Common issues which are found include:

- Are the questions unambiguous?
- Can respondents understand the language and terminology?

To address these issues, it is usual to identify a similar group of respondents to the one in the final survey. If carrying out a survey of surgical nurses, then it might be reasonable to pilot the questionnaire with a group of surgical nurses in a different hospital or a similar group in another directorate. The idea here is to avoid introducing bias into the sample group by pre-exposure to the questionnaire, or in layman's terms 'muddying the water'. This process is always extremely valuable, and it is common to find that even (in the researcher's mind) the most straightforward questions can be open to a number of interpretations, which will threaten the validity of the research. The pilot group does not have to be a large one, and as few as 10–12 individuals will do as long as their comments and suggestions are heeded and included in the final questionnaire. By this process it is common for the questionnaire to go through a number of developmental stages before finalisation, but this step is always necessary.

CHAPTER 7

Quantitative research: data analysis

Statistics is a branch of mathematics that deals with collecting, organising and interpreting data using systematic procedures. Surprisingly, it aims to simplify the data, not complicate them. Experience has shown that nurses, on the whole, make reluctant statisticians, but it is equally likely that statisticians would probably make terrible nurses. It is, however, true that statistics can be very, very complicated. Fortunately, the use of computers and statistical software packages has taken a lot of the hard work out of quantitative data analysis. Most people who have a computer run Microsoft Windows software. If you also have Microsoft Office, then you will have copy of Microsoft Excel. This can be used to explore data, and although Excel is widely used for fairly simple tasks such as keeping household budgets, it can be used in much more exciting ways. In this chapter it will be used to explore some examples of both descriptive and inferential statistics, to get the reader to interact with some data.

Most students who get involved with statistics in some way will want a more specialised tool, and there are a number available. SPSS is one of these which is widely used in the UK and USA. There are a number of guides for using it, and the best of these include data sets on CD or available online so that students can not only read about what to do, but can actually do it in real time. Two good examples are written by Argyrous (2005) and Field (2009). The former is an excellent starting point and would be likely to be adequate for degree- and masters-level work. Once you have been bitten by the bug and cannot stop, then Field's book will give you all the detail that you will ever need, and is the only book on statistical data analysis (so far) which is likely to make the reader laugh out loud.

Entering data in Excel

The examples here use the 2007 version of Excel. Earlier ones are very similar, but may require a little flexibility on behalf of the user.

When Excel is opened up, the main page is presented as a set of cells. Entering data is fairly straightforward: clicking on a cell allows the entry of data in either the cell itself or in the function dialogue box:

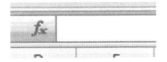

The two sets of data discussed below were developed from an exercise I have used with Learning Beyond Registration healthcare degree students.

Data set A is the heart rate of the students before a coffee break, when both their spirits and their physiology have been depressed listening to an interminable lecture on survey research. Set B is the same set of students immediately after a coffee break, when suitably loaded up with caffeine and/or nicotine they have returned to the lecture.

Excel exercise

Enter the following data into Excel, plus the titles at the foot of the columns. The data should look like this:

	Group A	Group B
	80	77
	89	86
	78	76
	76	99
	68	74
	92	67
	87	83
	93	87
	83	85
	84	87
	82	81
	84	89
	78	71
	86	95
	74	90
	77	96
	73	86
	96	92
	71	81
	64	79
Max		
Min		
Average		
Median		
Mode		
Sdev		
t test		

This chapter will introduce two main types of statistics, descriptive and inferential. It is always best to do the descriptive work first, followed by the inferential.

Descriptive statistics

These literally describe the population, so that a set of numbers can be described and summarised. Descriptive statistics are the essential first step in data analysis and although relatively straightforward are very valuable. Examples include:

- Frequencies, percentages, measures of central tendency; these are all numerical ways to present data
- Tables, charts; these are graphical ways to present data

For a survey they may be the only statistics required. Commonly, however, it is desirable or necessary to go further, for example to compare one population with another; the classic example would be for an experiment where it is necessary to compare values for two sets of dependent variables. Techniques such as these are termed inferential statistics.

Inferential statistics

These provide predictions about populations. They do more than describe data – they can predict behaviour between variables. Examples, which will be discussed later, include *t*-tests, **Analysis of Variance**, **Mann–Whitney** and **Kruskal–Wallis** tests, and others.

Descriptive statistics: what do the data look like?

Tables

Tables are commonly used to summarise frequencies, i.e. to count the number of cases in which a variable occurs. Here is an example from SPSS.

Marks as %

		Frequency	Percent	Valid percent	Cumulative percent
Valid	35	1	1.0	1.2	1.2
	40	5	5.2	5.9	7.1
	42	2	2.1	2.4	9.4
	43	4	4.2	4.7	14.1
	45	5	5.2	5.9	20.0
	46	1	1.0	1.2	21.2
	48	2	2.1	2.4	23.5
	49	1	1.0	1.2	24.7
	50	3	3.1	3.5	28.2
	51	1	1.0	1.2	29.4
	52	7	7.3	8.2	37.6
	55	6	6.2	7.1	44.7
	56	3	3.1	3.5	48.2
	58	11	11.5	12.9	61.2
	60	3	3.1	3.5	64.7
	61	1	1.0	1.2	65.9
	62	7	7.3	8.2	74.1
	63	1	1.0	1.2	75.3
	64	1	1.0	1.2	76.5
	65	4	4.2	4.7	81.2
	66	1	1.0	1.2	82.4
	68	6	6.2	7.1	89.4
	71	1	1.0	1.2	90.6
	72	6	6.2	7.1	97.6
	75	1	1.0	1.2	98.8
	80	1	1.0	1.2	100.0
	Total	85	88.5	100.0	
Missing	System	11	11.5		
Total		96	100.0		

The variable is the marks for a research module. The frequency is the number of students who scored that particular mark. The other headings are of less interest: the differences between *Percent* and *Valid percent* are caused by missing data, and the cumulative total always adds up to 100 per cent of the cases. This is a good example of SPSS output, in that not only does it give you the data you need, it also gives you quite a lot of stuff you do not!

Just doing this has helped display the data so that we can see the lowest, or minimum score (35%) and the highest or maximum (80%). In addition, we can see that there are higher frequencies between 52–60%, so we might expect the average score to be in this range.

Excel Example 2

As we have seen, a first step in exploring the Excel data is to put them in order. To do this, click and drag over the numbers in data set A; if you are unsure how to do this, ask any teenager! The spreadsheet will look like this:

Group A	Group B
80	77
89	86
78	76
76	99
68	74
92	67
87	83
93	87
83	85
84	87
82	81
84	89
78	71
86	95
74	90
77	96
73	86
96	92
71	81
64	79

Now go to the 'sort and filter' command on the taskbar at the top of the page. Click on the little arrow on the bottom right and you will be presented with a number of options. Click on the first 'Sort Smallest to Largest'; this will sort the table for you, so you can inspect the data, as we did for the marks table. Ignore invitations to 'expand the data', opt to continue with the current selection.

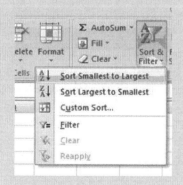

The table should now look like this:

Group A	Group B
64	77
68	80
71	76
73	99
74	74
76	67
77	83
78	87
78	85
80	87
82	81
83	89
84	71
84	95
86	90
87	96
89	86
92	92
93	81
96	79

Repeat the process for group B. Start to get a feel for the data. Are the maximums and minimums similar or different? Enter the values for maximum and minimum on the Excel spreadsheet.

Max	96	99
Min	64	67
Average		
Median		
Mode		
Sdeviation		
t test		

Where is the middle of the range? Having inspected the data, you may come to some conclusions as to which has the highest values, but it should already be obvious that more detail is necessary to explore even these small sets of data.

This exercise has shown that tables can be useful to summarise a set of data. It is unusual to display tables of a data set in a publication as they are quite cumbersome; instead charts may provide a more visual and readily accessible summary.

Charts

There are many different types of chart. Three commonly used are:

- Bar charts
- Histograms
- Pie charts

Bar chart

Having spent some time extolling the virtues of Excel, we will take one step back – Excel is good, but the graphics package which comes with it is not very flexible. Instead, for this section SPSS will be used to display examples of data.

Bar charts are one of the simplest charts. They are used to display nominal and ordinal data. Typically, the nominal variable is entered on the horizontal (or *x*) axis, to represent the grouping of the data, and the frequency of cases (if categorical) or mean values (if ordinal or interval) are represented by the vertical (or *y*) axis.

Figure 7.1 is an example of a bar chart.

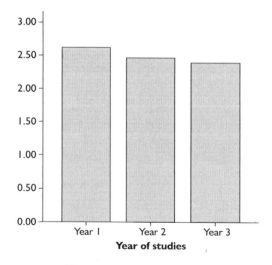

Figure 7.1 A bar chart.

This is taken from Norrie and Dalby (2007). In this study 318 pre-registration nursing students completed a survey, using a set of Likert scale statements, to explore their preferred ways of learning. The *y*-axis represents their willingness to manage their own learning and uses the average value (or mean, to be mathematically more accurate). The *x*-axis is grouped to show the year of study. This bar chart seems to show that as the students progressed through their studies they become more reluctant to manage their own learning, and hence behaved less like adult learners; a trait which was picked up by other statements in the questionnaire. A lot of data have therefore been usefully summarised here, so that a clear message has been produced. This does however need to be explored further, using both descriptive and inferential statistics.

Histograms

Histograms are similar to bar charts, but they are used where the data on the *x*-axis are continuous, so they must be at least ordinal. With a histogram, the data are grouped into blocks, so that each bar represents a range of data; for example, in Figure 7.2 each block represents a value of two marks.

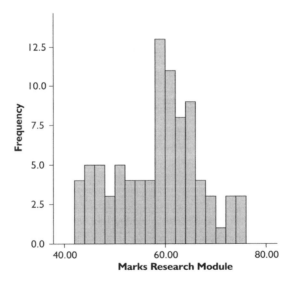

Figure 7.2 A histogram.

This is another set of marks, from yet another research module. This is clearly a superior way of looking at the data compared to a table. Here it can be seen that the main grouping lies between 58% and 66%, but that there is another grouping between 44% and 50%. This is, however, open to interpretation (is there also a high scoring group?) and illustrates that showing the data in a chart, although useful, has its limitations.

Pie chart

A pie chart is a circle which has been partitioned into percentage groups of nominal or ordinal variables. It is a very clear way of providing an overview of the population. If there are more than six variables it may become too cluttered (Munro, 2001).

Here is an example taken from a masters degree project which was subsequently published (Norrie, 1997). In this research, nurses working in an Intensive Cardiothoracic Unit were asked to log how they spent their time, at the end of each hour, using five activity descriptors. Figure 7.3 shows these data as a pie chart.

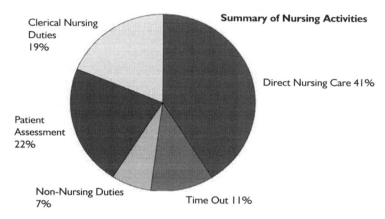

Figure 7.3 A pie chart.

The pie chart shows clearly that the majority of their time was spent working in appropriate activities, three slices of the pie – Direct Nursing Care, Patient Assessment and Clerical Nursing Duties – together adding up to 82% of the nurses' time, and these figures were used to support the nursing management structures used at that time.

Box plots

The final chart to be explored is the box plot (Figure 7.4). Box plots are useful because they clearly show differences between populations. They are based upon the use of percentiles.

This box plot is part of the results from a research project exploring the achievement of Asian students in an English university during their nursing diplomas and degrees (Dyson *et al.*, 2008).

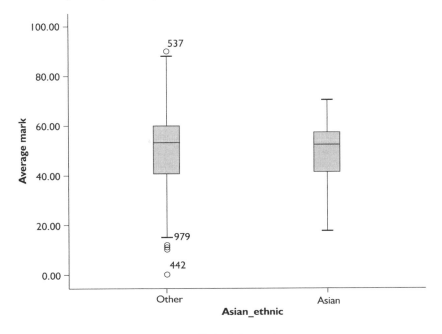

Figure 7.4 A box plot.

There are two groups shown for comparison. One is 'Other', representing the non-Asian students, a mix of predominantly white and smaller numbers of black students, and the other group is students who described themselves as 'Asian'. The average marks for their studies over a period of three years are shown on the left side. The chart shows:

- **The median**: this is the bar in the middle of the boxes. It is a measurement of central tendency, and is one way to summarise what the main characteristic of the population is. In everyday terms we might describe this as an 'average' (although, as shall be shown, this is not strictly correct). If you look closely at the median values, it can be seen that the 'Other' group has a slightly higher value than the 'Asian,' suggesting that they get slightly better marks, overall.
- **The boxes**: the shaded area above the medians shows where the first 25% of the population above the median lie, and the shaded area below shows where the first 25% of the population below the median lie. These are termed percentiles, and will be familiar to any health professional who deals with growth and development in children. Thus the first 50% of the population is summarised within the boxes.
- **The tails**: populations spread out from the central values, and the tails pick up the remaining 25% above and 25% below the 50% grouping. There are a number of outliers (these have data set numbers attached to them, so that we

can check they have been entered correctly); these are values which SPSS has identified as falling outside of the main population and as being 'odd'.

The box plot allows us to compare the two groups. Basically they look quite similar, but both the median and first 25% above the median of the 'Other' grouping are slightly higher, so as a first step in analysis it may be thought that the 'Other' students do slightly better than the 'Asian' ones. What this does not show is whether this is a real difference which can be used with confidence to predict future outcomes. To do this it is necessary to use statistics to explore the group.

In summary, although tables can be a useful preliminary to sorting and inspecting data sets, the use of charts further simplifies and illustrates the process. Even so, charts have limitations and it is necessary to start to use statistical techniques to explore the information hidden in the numbers.

Excel exercise

Figure 7.5 shows the box plots for the Excel heart rate data: what can you tell from them? Does it make a case for a difference between populations, and if so, which group has the higher values?

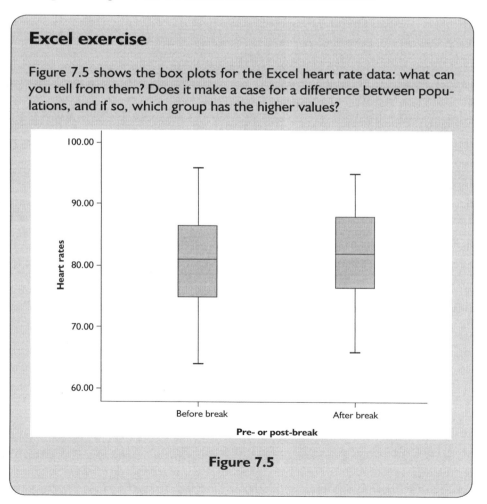

Figure 7.5

Looking at populations

Charts allow us to inspect the data we are interested in. Here are the histograms for the Excel data, entered into SPSS. SPSS has overlaid a very characteristic shape on the charts. This classic bell shape is termed the normal or parametric population. Figures 7.6 and 7.7 show the histograms for populations A and B.

The normal population is important because if the data correspond to a normal population (i.e. can honestly be described as being approximately 'normal'), then a number of predictions can be made. This is important in statistical analysis.

A normal population:

■ has a characteristic bell shaped curve
■ is symmetrical
■ encompasses almost all the data set

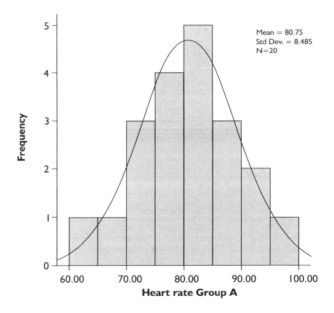

Mean = 80.75
Std Dev. = 8.485
N=20

Heart rate Group A

Figure 7.6

Excel exercise

Review the histograms for the two populations. Do they look normal? Justify your decision.

Analysis

Inspection of charts such as these is one way of assessing whether a population follows the normal distribution. There is a problem, however, because for statisticians it is quite desirable for their population to be normal, as this allows advanced statistical techniques to be used. This means there is a possibility of bias, and indeed it has been shown that people who publish healthcare research tend to make this assumption, often without justification (Anthony, 1996). For the statistically minded, the Kolmogorov–Smirnov test can be applied to the data to give a much more robust estimate. Using it for both these sets of data, it can be confirmed that they are indeed normally distributed.

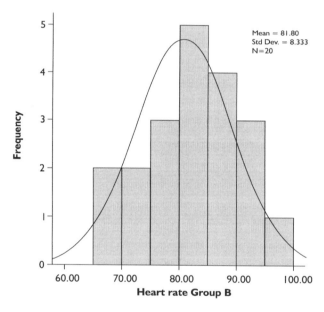

Figure 7.7

Terminology

Most textbooks describe the characteristic bell-shaped curve as being 'normal'. If the population does not fit this shape it is commonly said to be 'not normal'. There is a problem here for researchers interested in healthcare, where we try to be inclusive. There is an inference here that subjects who do not fit within the normal distribution are 'not normal'. For example if we are exploring intelligence, then a small number of people will always fall outside the normal distribution, but it is ugly terminology to describe them as being 'not normal'. This sort of terminology was used by the eugenics movement in the early 20th century, which had views on race that are really not acceptable in the 21st century. There is, fortunately, an alternative. The normal population can also be said to be **parametric**, which means that it adheres to the parameters or characteristics identified above. Populations which do not conform to these parameters are said to be *non-parametric*, and these are the terms which will be used from now on.

Central tendency

So far, we have reviewed a number of ways to get a feel for data. It is now necessary to be more precise. Researchers are commonly interested in the idea of measuring the central tendency of a population. This is the number which best summarises the main body of the data. In everyday usage we might say that 'on average' I drink 20 units of alcohol per week, or smoke 20 cigarettes per day. Clearly, when exploring data sets it is necessary to be more precise than this. There are three main ways to represent central tendency:

■ **Average or mean**
The mean is the true mathematical average of the population. All the values in a population are added together and divided by the number of cases. The mean is probably the most widely accepted and understood measure of central tendency, but it has limitations. It can be affected by a small number of extreme scores. For this reason it works well with a parametric population, but should be treated with some caution in a non-parametric one.

■ **Median**
This is the middle value of a set of ordered numbers. Imagine that we have 21 people in a room, and we arrange them in a line so that the smallest is on one end and the tallest on the other end. The person who is in the middle is the median. 10 people will be taller (50% of the population will lie above the median) and 10 will be shorter (50% of the population will lie below the median). In fact, with this small set of data there are some inconsistencies: having chosen one person as the median, this then reduces the percentage above and below, but in practice this is not a problem, as most data sets are much larger. This method is much more resistant to extreme cases than the mean and so is commonly used with non-parametric populations.

■ Mode

This is the simplest of all measures of central tendency. It is not calculated at all, it is spotted. It is the most frequent value or category in a data set. Some non-parametric populations, far from having an elegant bell-shaped distribution, are decidedly lumpy, and so may have a number of peaks or modes – these are described as multimodal distributions.

Excel exercise

Excel can be used to identify the three measures of central tendency. Click on the cell next to 'average'; this tells the computer where you want the results to be delivered.

Max	96	99
Min	64	67
Average		
Median		
Mode		
Sdev		
t test		

Next, click on the small arrow on the right of 'AutoSum' in the toolbar. This produces a short menu. Click on 'average'.

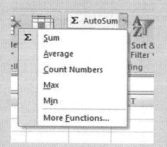

The computer will automatically select a set of numbers, but ignore this. Click and drag over the first data set (A) like this (the row and column selection numbers may vary, but this does not matter):

	Group A	Group B	
	64	67	
	68	71	
	71	74	
	73	76	
	74	77	
	76	79	
	77	81	
	78	81	
	78	83	
	80	85	
	82	86	
	83	86	
	84	87	
	84	87	
	86	89	
	87	90	
	89	92	
	92	95	
	93	96	
	96	99	

Max	96	99
Min	64	67
Average	=AVERAGE(D6:D25)	
Median	AVERAGE(number1, [numb	
Mode		

Now press 'enter' on your keyboard, and the average will appear!

Max	96	99
Min	64	67
Average	80.75	
Median		
Mode		
Sdev		
t test		

This is the basic technique for running samples in Excel, so it is worth getting your technique perfect. Work out the average for group B.

Medians and modes are found by using the same technique; click on the space for the median for set A. It is now necessary to go into the AutoSum command, as before, and click on the 'More Functions' tab. A dialogue box appears and you can then type 'Median' in the 'Search for a Function' window.

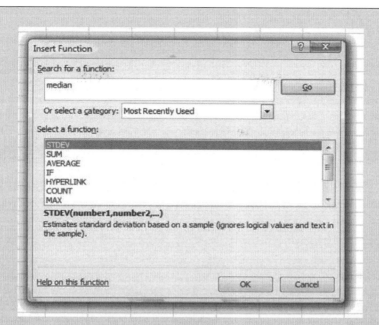

Click on 'Go', and repeat the process of highlighting the individual data sets. Once highlighted, click on 'OK'. The computer will automatically select the data it thinks you want to analyse, but it is always better to select your own (it does have some strange ideas at times). Repeat for set B and to find the modes for both sets.

The table should now look like this:

Max	96	99
Min	64	67
Average	80.75	84.05
Median	81	85.5
Mode	78	81
Sdev		
t test		

This a good time to compare the means, medians and modes. We already know that these populations are parametric, therefore the mean is the main indicator of central tendency we would use. The mean in set B is higher; suggesting that the students, following their coffee break had higher heart rates. This finding is supported by examination of the median and mode, which show a similar difference.

Standard deviation

The data so far seem to indicate that group B has a higher heart rate than group A, but before accepting this, there is some more information which we need.

Standard deviation measures the spread of a population. If we wish to compare populations, we not only need to know the measure of central tendency, but we also need to know how far the population spreads above and below the mean. This is calculated by subtracting each variable from the mean, the result is then squared, summed and divided by the number of individuals in the population, and then the square root is taken. Ideally SD should only be used in populations which are parametric (but they do crop up elsewhere).

Excel exercise

We can calculate SD using Excel. As before, click on the cell where you wish the data to be recorded for group A's SD:

Max	96	99
Min	64	67
Average	80.75	84.05
Median	81	85.5
Mode	78	81
Sdev		
t test		

Next click on the little triangular tab at the right of the AutoSum box. It will show some options:

Click on More Functions. A dialogue box will come up. You can either look through the various menus, or simply type in STDEV (as shown below), then click Go.

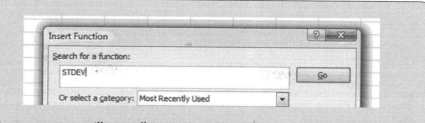

The computer will actually present you with a number of slightly different ways to calculate SD. We will use the most straightforward one, 'STDEV'. Click on OK at the bottom of the box. A new window should now open up:

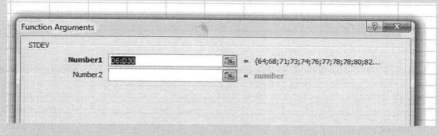

This is the prompt to either enter the letter and number for the cells you wish to calculate SD for, or to click and drag over the set of numbers in Column A. When you have done this click OK in the function box, and the SD should appear on your spreadsheet:

This gives a SD of 8.48 (it is a standard scientific convention that only the first two decimal points are given).

We now have a value for mean and standard deviation of population A. What does this tell us?

Take a piece of paper and draw a bell-shaped curve as shown in Figure 7.8.

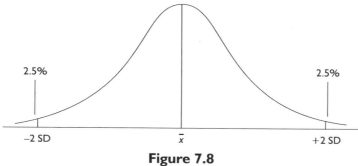

Figure 7.8

Write the mean where the letter X is. To the mean, add two times the standard deviation: the mean for population A is 80.75 (i.e. approximately 80); the SD is 8.5, therefore the upper figure here is 97. Write this in where it says +2SD.

Now repeat this, but subtract two times the SD from the mean and write it in too. Within these two limits approximately 95% of the population lies. These are commonly referred to as confidence limits, because it means we can be confident that this is where most of the population lies. Conversely only 2.5% of the population exists above the confidence limit and 2.5% below it. This is not just an academic discussion. With a mean and the SD, it is possible to summarise any parametric population, and as will be shown next these are one of the key concepts behind statistical testing. To be precise, the confidence limits are the mean plus or minus 1.96 times SD, but 2 is a useful approximation.

Inferential statistics: testing the differences between groups

Figure 7.9 shows two hypothetical populations. These could might be two groups of surgical patients, of which Group A had a standard form of post-operative analgesia and Group B had a new experimental one.

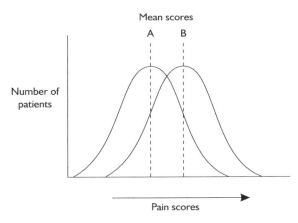

Figure 7.9

The figure summarises the pain scores for the two groups. Look at the graph; is it possible to distinguish between the two populations? Do they look significantly different?

Inspection would seem to suggest that if a patient was in group A, they are more likely to have a lower pain score than if they were in group B. There is, however, a lot of overlap, so there are a lot of people for whom it does not matter which group they were in, they had similar pain scores. In statistical terms, it is unlikely that they would have a significantly different pain score, regardless of which group they were in. In layman's terms, although it looks as though group A had a lower set of scores, the chart alone cannot show whether the groups were really different.

Now look at the populations in Figure 7.10.

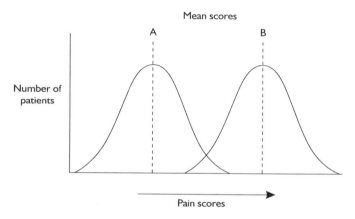

Figure 7.10

It is a similar picture, but this time there is very little overlap between the two groups. Still using the pain scenario outlined above, it looks as if almost everyone within group B has a higher pain score, with very little overlap between the two. This suggests that there is a real difference between the groups, and you may consider that, if given the choice, it would be a good idea to sign up to group A.

What these examples show is that when comparing two populations, it is necessary not only to compare measures of central tendency (means, medians and modes), but also to compare the spread of the populations (standard deviations). The branch of statistics which explores these connections between groups is termed inferential statistics.

The classic inferential test to compare two populations is Student's *t*-test. It is only applicable if a population is parametric. A *t*-test compares the two populations and determines whether they can be seen to be statistically separated. It looks at the mean and the spread of the population and compares these to a completely random population.

Examples of unpaired tests could include:

- Using a quantitative questionnaire to score differences in stress between men and women
- Comparing percentage marks for a group of students taught using a distance learning package with a group using conventional methods
- Number of days survival of patients following myocardial infarction between those treated with thrombolysis and those with rescue angioplasty

Not all sets of data can be assessed this way. Firstly, the independent variable must be at least of interval level and both populations should be parametric. Lastly, the populations should have similar variance, which really means that the populations should look fairly similar (as in the examples above).

t-tests can also be paired or unpaired. Unpaired tests explore populations where the individuals cannot be identified. Paired tests explore the population where the same individuals are measured twice. Paired tests are more powerful, meaning that they have a greater ability to identify differences between groups.

Excel exercise

This is the final use of Excel to explore statistics, and it is the most complex. Make sure that you have mastered the previous examples. As before, click on the cell where you would like the result for the *t*-test to appear.

Max	96	99
Min	64	67
Average	80.75	84.05
Median	81	85.5
Mode	78	81
Sdev	8.48451	8.450942
t test		

Now, in the same way that you looked for the STDEV function in the Auto sum dialogue box, go into More Functions and find TTEST. Click on this in the 'Select a function' box:

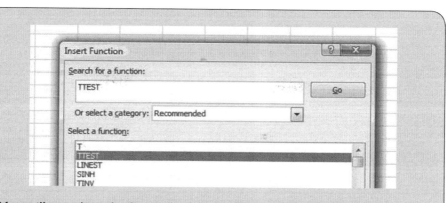

You will now be asked to enter two arrays of data. Click and drag over data set A and its location should appear in the first array box.

Repeat for the second array. Both sets of data have now been entered (the cell numbers will vary according to where you put your original data). There are two final dialog boxes:

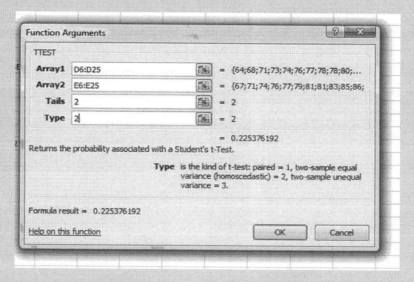

We will assume that there are two tails to this test (this means it is possible for one group to be higher *or* lower than the other) and it is a type two test we want where the variances for the two groups are similar, as we know that related statistics, the standard deviations, are similar . Then click OK. The result for the *t*-test should appear like this:

Max	96	99
Min	64	67
Average	80.75	84.05
Median	81	85.5
Mode	78	81
Sdev	8.484506002	7.05279
t test	0.225376192	

Just before we interpret the *t*-test, there is one final point to consider.

Statistical significance

When we inspected the charts comparing pain relief, we found that it was not possible to say that one set of data was absolutely different from the other. If pressed, it might be possible to say that in the second example, one was *very probably* different from the other. The same is true when we run inferential statistics such as a *t*-test. The test will not say that 'set A is definitely different from set B'; instead it gives a probability, also known as a *p* value.

The smaller the *p* value, the more likely it is that two sets of data are different. Scientists use a *p*-value of 0.05 as the cut off. If a *p* value is 0.05, it means that in 5% (this is another way of writing 0.05) of the cases, the test may get it wrong, but the other 95% of the times the test is run, it has picked up a real difference between groups.

The Excel example which we ran gave a *p* value of 0.22. This is much larger than 0.05, so although the measures of central tendency are all lower for set A, the two sets of data are not statistically different at all! This means that if these data were the result of an experiment, the researchers would have to conclude that there was no real difference between the two treatments. Incidentally, although the cut-off point of 0.05 is universally used, it is actually only a convention. It was introduced by a statistician called Ronald Fisher in the 1920s and since then has been widely adopted. As Field (2009) has pointed out, if Fisher had woken up one day with a '0.10' feeling, the whole course of science might have been different!

Other tests

t-tests only work when there are two groups. If there are more than two samples then Analysis of Variance (ANOVA) may be suitable. This test assumes that all groups are equal and drawn from the same population. As with *t*-tests, the independent or grouping variable is nominal but must have more than two levels: for example gender has two levels (so would require a *t*-test); ethnicity, however, has many levels, so if it is desirable to see whether there are differences between groups in a survey, ANOVA would be used. The output is similar, providing *p* numbers between groups.

Fisher was a very busy man, and in addition to determining the significance level, he invented ANOVA and also an entirely new field of inferential statistics: the use of *non-parametric* techniques. As the name suggests these are used where a population does not have not the classic bell-shaped curve.

These tests make fewer assumptions and are generally held to be less powerful, but they are very valuable, particularly in small research projects.

As before, the first step in data analysis would be consideration of the nature of the population. If it cannot be confirmed that the population is para-

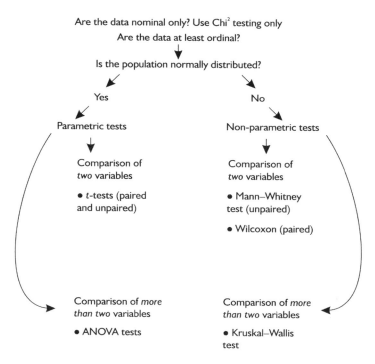

Figure 7.11 Quantitative data tests.

metric, then non-parametric techniques are used. If there are two independent groups, then the Mann–Whitney U test would be used, whereas if there are more than two independent groups, then the Kruskal–Wallis test would be used. These techniques work in a different way from the parametric tests. Rather than comparing means and distribution, the scores are put into ranks. The analysis then compares the ranks. However, the outcome is very similar: a probability is produced and, as before, if the result is smaller than 0.05 then the test groups are statistically different. Figure 7.11 (p. 105) shows a flow chart of the commonly used statistical tests.

Chi square test

This is the final test to be considered. The preceding discussion has been focused on data which are at least ordinal, and ideally would be interval. However, in health research, quite commonly the outcomes are categorical; for example live or dead, pregnant or not!

If the outcome of a piece of research is categorical and there are two groups involved, then the suitable technique to distinguish between groups is the Chi (pronounced 'kye') square test. An example from Argyrous (2005) is shown below:

Place of residence	Low income	High income
Rural	205	118
Urban	167	230

The question here is whether there is a link between place of residence and income. For example, it might be thought that poor people tend to live in inner city areas and the well-off live in large villas in the country. Is this what is represented here? This sort of table is termed a cross-tabulation and summarises the data clearly. The Chi square test assumes that the two headings (place and income) are not related, it assumes independence between the variables. As usual it is always a good idea to look at the descriptive data. If these are summarised as percentages, the data appear as:

Place of residence	Low income	High income
Rural	55%	34%
Urban	45%	66%

Inspection shows that those on low income actually seem to be over-represented in the rural environment (55%) rather than the urban (45%). If the same pattern exists for the high-income group then there is probably no difference between high- and low-income groups, or income is independent of residence. But if (for example) a greater number of high earners live in urban areas, this may show that residence is related to income, so income is not independent of residence. Inspection seems to show that there are fewer people from the high-income bracket in the rural environment (34%) rather than the urban (66%). The groups therefore seem to be behaving differently, but is this difference statistically significant? Running a Chi Square test on this set of data gives a p value of <0.001. This means less than 1 in 1000. Clearly this is much smaller than 0.05, so the answer is that these populations are really different: the low-income families are really more likely to live in the rural environment and the high-income ones in the urban (and vice versa).

This is rather a brief discussion on the use of categorical data, but there is a reason for this. In this example, the terms 'low and 'high' income are not defined. With more detailed data, for example income considered in annual bands such as £0–5,000, £5,000–10,000 etc., it is possible to be more detailed in the analyses. These data are now interval level, and so (for example) could produce all the descriptive data already discussed and could be distinguished by either a t or Mann–Whitney test, depending on the distribution of the population.

As a general rule, it is recommended that when constructing questionnaires, you should aim for the highest form of data that can be accessed as this will allow the most detailed analysis.

An introduction to statistical relationships

The statistical techniques explored so far have focused on finding out whether groups can be demonstrated to be different. This is very important, for example in determining whether two groups in an experiment show real changes to client outcomes; this could illustrate the effect of a new drug or a new nursing intervention. This is, however, only a start; this final section of the chapter can be viewed as a further 'taster' of what statistics can do. Rather than look for differences, statistics can be used to identify relationships (Sapsford, 2007) between variables, which is also termed modelling. This branch of enquiry can give more insight into the relationship between data sets.

Correlations

The most basic technique, but also one of the most important, is to look for correlations between variables. Figure 7.12 uses another type of chart, a scatter plot, to show the relationship between pain and anxiety in a set of post-operative patients:

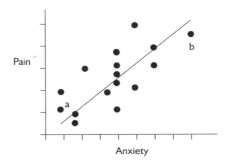

Figure 7.12 A scatter plot.

It can be seen here that as anxiety score increases, the pain score also increases. For example, patient 'a' has an anxiety score of one and a pain score of one also. Patient 'b' is less fortunate: he or she has an anxiety score of 8 and also a pain score of between 4 and 5. This is an example of a positive correlation: as one score increases, the other decreases. It is not a perfect relationship. The drawn line shows the direction of the correlation, but not all data lie on the line. To explore these further, as with techniques for exploring differences between data sets, it is necessary to determine whether the data are parametrically or non-parametrically distributed. If the distribution can be shown to be parametrically distributed, then Pearson's Correlation can be used.

Running a Pearson's Correlation gives two statistics. The first is the correlation statistic, which is a value between -1 and 1. Since we can be sure that this is a positive relationship, in this case the number for these data will be between 0 and 1. A score of 1 is a perfect correlation, and in this case all the data would appear on the drawn line. A score of 0 would mean that there was no relationship at all. The other statistic is the level of probability. This has been discussed before, and the same cut-off of a value less than 0.05 is used here. Microsoft Excel does not analyse for correlations, so a more sophisticated statistical package such as SPSS would be used here.

For these data, the output from SPSS would be:

Pearson correlation= 0.85
$p= 0.002$

This shows that there is a strong positive correlation between the two data sets, and that it is statistically significant. This means we can be confident in saying that as anxiety score increases, so does the patient's pain. What it *does not do* is show that one causes the other, i.e. we do not know if the pain causes the anxiety, or the anxiety causes the pain (or possibly a mix of the two).

If these were non-parametric data, then correlation would be explored by Spearman's rho. In practice, although possibly less sensitive, the same format of result is given, a *rho* value between −1 and 1 and a *p* value.

Figure 7.13 shows an example of a negative correlation.

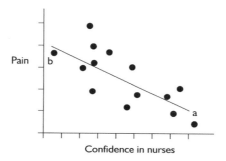

Figure 7.13 Negative correlation.

Here a different picture emerges. Patient 'a' has a high measure of confidence in the nurses and a low pain score, whereas patient 'b' is again unfortunate: he or she has almost no confidence in the nurses and a high pain score. With a negative correlation, as one index rises, the other falls. This is again summarised with the drawn line. Assuming that these data are not parametrically distributed, then Spearman's correlation would be the appropriate choice for exploring the correlation.

For these data, the output from SPSS would be:

Spearman's *rho* = −0.5
p = 0.03

The negative value of the *rho* shows clearly that this is a negative correlation. It can be seen here that, in addition to it being negative, the correlation is not as large as the previous example. This means that fewer of the data are summarised by the correlation statistic coefficient. This is a moderate correlation, but as the *p* value shows it is still statistically significant. This means that we can confirm a negative correlation between pain and confidence in the nurses, but as before we cannot comment on causality.

The Pearson correlation statistic and Spearman's rho are both correlation coefficients: they explain the relationship between the two variables. One final refinement is to square these values, to show the amount of data that is explained by the correlation (Field, 2009).

For example 1, which we have identified as having a strong positive correlation, this is 0.85×0.85, which equals 0.72, or 72% of the data, i.e. only 28% of the data are not explained by the correlation.

For example 2, a moderate negative correlation, this is -0.5×-0.5, which equals 0.25, which therefore accounts for only 25% of the data. Note that the negative value becomes lost when the negative correlation is multiplied by itself.

Other modelling techniques

These produce sophisticated models and are not for the faint hearted!

They can be summarised as using predictor variables which explain an outcome variable. An example can be found in Fowler and Norrie (2009), which explored why students might consider leaving their programme of nursing studies.

The *outcome variable* was a question: 'Since starting your programme of studies, have you ever thought seriously about resigning or leaving the course?', which was scored using a Likert scale. A set of predictor variables was given, composed of 27 items which might realistically have an effect on this outcome (for example 'I am finding the volume of work to be too much'). To explore this, a modelling technique called multiple regression was used, which produced a model showing that eight of these variables accounted for 33% of the variation within the data. These predictors were then used, with the addition of qualitative data, to produce a tool which is being used currently to support students who are at risk of leaving their studies. This can be seen as an extension of correlational statistics.

One final technique to mention is logistic regression, which measures the chances of an event happening similarly using a set of predictors (see Table 7.1).

Table 7.1 Summary of levels of data in regression analyses.

Technique	Outcome variable	Predictor variables
Multiple regression	At least ordinal	At least ordinal
Logistic regression	Dichotomous nominal	Nominal or ordinal

Although mathematically different from multiple regression, in practice it produces similar types of findings. It is mentioned here because it is used commonly by medical researchers. As you can see from Table 7.1, the outcome variable is dichotomous (two possible choices) and nominal only, e.g. yes or no. This can be useful in medical studies where the outcomes are similarly nominal, e.g. in renal failure (or not), or allergic or not.

These techniques allow quite sophisticated and robust modelling, but again, they cannot show causality. Lastly, beware of statistical techniques like these because they are addictive. You have been warned!

CHAPTER 8

Other strategies and evidence

This is the final chapter of the book. It will pull together some of the themes which have been explored so far, and it will introduce a final one. This is the concept of 'evidence', and the aim is to explore some aspects of what evidence-based practice means for nurses. Two important sources of evidence have already been introduced; these are research findings which may have been produced by both qualitative and quantitative enquiry.

These two branches have so far been explored separately. This is a useful strategy when introducing the world of research. However, the split between the two can be overstated. A growing number of researchers are using both branches to produce findings relevant to practice. A common method is to start out with inductive (i.e. qualitative) methods to identify the phenomena of interest. This is because qualitative work seldom answers questions, but instead produces new theory. In layperson's terms this means it generates new ideas. This is positive, but the researcher may feel that the work is unfinished, and instead may wish to measure how important, or otherwise, these ideas are in the world of practice. The clue here is in the word 'quantify'; to do this, it is logical to also use deductive (i.e. quantitative) methods (Teddlie and Tashakkori, 2009). Here is an example to work through.

Exercise: Tackling the paperwork

Your clinical area has invested £500,000 in an advanced electronic patient data management system. When fully implemented this will result in a 'paperless' ward environment, and it is hoped that this will liberate time for medical staff and nurses, which can then be spent in delivering patient care.

A lecturer at a local university is keen to participate in the evaluation of this project and will participate in the fieldwork and data analysis, on the understanding that this can be used for a PhD project.

Identify how many research investigations you will include

A part time PhD usually lasts five years. Realistically this will result in fieldwork which can span a period of two years, during which the system will come on line.

Identify how you would structure the project, bearing in mind that very little has been written about the ways in which health workers use these systems. Include some pre- and post-implementation measures.

Will there be one or more quantitative phases, one or more qualitative phases, or a mix of both?

Discussion
There are many different ways in which this research could have been undertaken. What actually happened was as follows.

A set of interviews was conducted in the clinical area where the system was going to be introduced. The main focus of these was asking the nurses what they wanted from the information system, and what their concerns might be. This therefore was an inductive stage. These findings were compared to a similar clinical area where they previously had used a computerised information system, which had then been discontinued. This allowed an analysis which identified common themes. These themes were then taken and used to construct a 23 item Likert scale, which was used in three clinical areas: two which used conventional manual data recording methods, and one which used a computerised system manufactured by Hewlett-Packard called CareVue. The result of this was that the research identified quite strongly that the computerised system gave consistently higher scores than manual recording in terms of reliability, time saving and communication. As good PhD students should, these were published shortly after completion of the project as Norrie (2003) and Norrie and Anthony (2004).

In many ways this is a fairly typical PhD project, and does indeed follow the inductive, then deductive format identified above. Taken together these findings form a set of evidence which could influence decision making regarding purchase of such a system.

Case studies

A case study usually investigates a topic within a real life setting. Therefore there are two conditions. Firstly the physical setting is (usually) clearly stated; for example, the research could take place within a community district, a ward or an operating department. If required, the case could actually be visited. Secondly, there is a technical or care-related issue which is to be investigated within this setting. In the example given above, it was the introduction of a computerised data system, but the opportunities are endless: the topic could be communication between nursing staff, wound management or attitudes to managing patients' complaints.

In research terms, Yin (2009) described the case study as a strategy for research, rather than a tradition, framework or paradigm. This means that rather than be tied to a particular way of doing the research (for example 'I am a qualitative researcher!'), the investigator can choose whichever methods work best for a particular part of the case study project. This gives a lot of freedom to workers and is therefore a popular way to proceed. This was confirmed by Bryar (1999), who reviewed a number of nursing case study projects and found that the majority used both qualitative and quantitative investigations within a geographically delineated area.

As well as being attractive, case studies can produce very good quality research. In good quality case studies, each step taken is demonstrated as being derived from the previous one, and this clear audit trail supports both reliability and validity. The case study has one special attribute: the clear and detailed description of a case can have an impact greater than almost any other form of research report (Gillham, 2000b). Perhaps for these reasons, the case study lends itself well to students undertaking doctorates, where the process of including multiple sources of information, making logical and justifiable steps in the chain of evidence, lends itself well to the format of an 80,000 word dissertation (Norrie, 2004).

A clear process is therefore required and a number of decisions have to be made to use a case study well. The researcher should:

1. Define the case, i.e. where is the study taking place and why
2. Identify the research tools which are best suited to the research questions
3. Carry out the fieldwork
4. Analyse the fieldwork
5. Decide if more fieldwork is needed; if so, repeat steps 2–5 again
6. Integrate the findings through a process of triangulation or mixed methods synthesis

Participatory action research (PAR): a 'hands on' tradition

This topic has been introduced earlier under qualitative methods, but is reintroduced here because it also allows the integration of a number of different types of research investigation.

All the discussions on quantitative methods so far have been based upon the positivist paradigm. This includes, albeit tacitly, the premise that the research is distinct from the research setting. For example, experiments are typically designed outside of the clinical area, and conducted by researchers who actually make a point of blinding the practitioners involved as to the nature of the experimental interventions they administer, in order to minimise the introduction of bias. The unwritten expectation is that research is done by 'others'; experts from outside the clinical area who can make dispassionate observations and analyses. The extreme case of this would be the Multi Centre Randomised Controlled Trial, where the researcher may be in a different country from where some (or all) of the fieldwork takes place.

As has been discussed, PAR is a response to this divorcing of research from the clinical area (McNiff and Whitehead, 2005). It is emancipatory, that is, it frees clinical staff to set their own research agendas and to use their knowledge in advancing the research (Morton-Cooper 2000). They are then no longer subjects of the research: they become the investigators! It is easy to see why nurses and other practitioners could get excited about PAR: for once, they can become the key players and are not reliant upon 'expert' researchers.

According to Denscombe (2007), action research has four main defining characteristics.

1. It is practical: it is aimed at dealing with real world issues within clinical settings. The research is undertaken as part of practice and is not distinct from it. The researchers are partners in the clinical area where care takes place.
2. It involves change: the practitioners are required to focus on their own practice as they engage in that practice. As with case studies, many different methods can be included, as long as they are a good fit for the research needs.
3. It is a cyclical process. The research includes a feedback loop. After (1) reflection on practice, (2) planning of change and (3) acting upon the plan comes (4) observation, before the team decides that the cycle is either complete (their goal has been achieved) or another turn of the cycle is required (their goal has not been achieved).
4. It is participative. Practitioners are the crucial people in the research process. Partnership is therefore a key process in action research. This is a radical revision of the relationship between researchers and subjects. Like case studies, it encourages the use of a variety of research methods including:
   – Reflective tools
   – Audit studies
   – Focus groups
   – Patient feedback surveys

It is included in this section because at the planning stage a number of options become available. In the words of Gilbert and Sullivan in the comic opera, the Mikado, 'let the punishment fit the crime'. Translated to the world of research, this means that the research questions should dictate the methods to be employed, and as with case studies these can be wide ranging. This perspective is close to the case study outlook, and indeed the action researcher might go further, using not only what may be termed 'accepted' research methods such as interviews and surveys, but more borderline ones too, for example clinical audit and client satisfaction surveys. This is particularly true where rapid appraisal of the issues is required. Murray and Graham (2009) cite the case of rapid appraisal of health needs of a group of residents in Scotland; the project combined document searches, new fieldwork using qualitative methods, hospital records and a postal survey. This collection would not look out of place in a case study approach, and indeed Denscombe (2007) links action research with case studies in terms of their reliability and validity. The differences are clear however; with PAR it is the participants within the clinical area who undertake the research and the emphasis is on change, action and evaluation the results of the action.

Bringing sets of data together

Whichever way the project is run, the output remains a number of sets of data. At some point, these have to be brought together to produce a set of findings which will summarise the project and produce findings which can be put into practice. What options are available?

Triangulation

Until recently the most frequently cited way to bring different sets of findings together was through a process called triangulation, publicised by Denzin and Lincoln (2000). This is a technical term used in surveying and navigation. Its principle is illustrated in Figure 8.1. On a flat surface, if two bearings are known then the position of a third point can be identified.

The inference here is that where the findings from the two sets of data cross over, the true findings will be found. There is a lot to be said for triangulation,

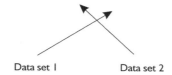

Data set 1　　　Data set 2

Figure 8.1 Triangulation.

in that it allows very different sets of data to be included in a research project. Distinctions have been made between many different types of triangulation, for example **within methods triangulation**, where two sets of methodologically similar data such as interviews are brought together, or **between methods triangulation**, where different types of data such as quantitative data from a questionnaire are compared with qualitative data from a focus group.

There are, however, problems with triangulation which has made it less frequently cited. First, it can be expensive. If the first piece of research answered the research question, it then becomes pointless to spend money on further investigations; the message here would be to formulate a sound piece of research in the first place. Different types of research may give completely different types of result; therefore there may not be any common ground at all between them (Sim and Sharp, 1998).

It is now more common to talk in terms of **Mixed Methods**, which may be typified as research projects which contain both quantitative and qualitative investigations. O'Cathain *et al.* (2007) identified that 18% of health service research studies could be classified as using mixed methods, and there was even evidence that despite being diehard quantitative researchers, medical staff had started using mixed methods because they were believed to attract funding! The main driver for using mixed methods is to make research more comprehensive, with the acknowledgement that healthcare takes place in complex environments, and is commonly involved with disempowered groups. One example might be clients with profound learning disabilities, who have difficulties in requesting what they need and whose voice may not be heard in a typical quantitative research structure. Mixed methods are therefore used widely in:

- Evaluation research, where the quality of a service is explored
- Surveys, where a large variety of clients are reached
- Experimental research, where qualitative data are obtained to add context to the main project findings

The 'added value' of these mixed methods is that rather than obtaining one agreed set of findings (as in triangulation), a breadth of findings are found, and it is the differences between data which are at least as valuable as the similarities. This will result in a **meta-inference**. To introduce some of the ways to do this, it will be assumed that there is one research project which has both a quantitative and a qualitative arm. Teddlie and Tashakkori's (2009) classification will be used.

1. **Parallel mixed data analysis**, where the separate data sets are analysed separately. The two sets of data are largely kept separate during the analysis. The understanding of the phenomenon under study is combined and linked together at a later stage. However, given that the researchers are

likely to be immersed in both aspects of the research project, early findings will shape the analysis of both or either arms.

2. **Sequential mixed data analysis** occurs where the different strands occur in chronological order, e.g. quantitative and *then* qualitative methods, and when the analysis of the first affects the analysis of the second. This is related to **iterative sequential mixed analysis**, which occurs in designs with more than two phases. Iteration means to repeat; in this context it means to return to the analysis on a number of occasions until a harmonious outcome is produced.

3. **Multilevel mixed data analysis**: occurs within research settings such as institutions where there is a hierarchy, for example a ward within a directorate, within a hospital or within an NHS Trust. It occurs where one type of research (for example a set of interviews with patients) is followed by another research method (for example exploring a set of patient satisfaction scores), moving up through the steps of the hierarchy.

4. **Fully integrated mixed data analysis**: occurs where a project uses a number of strands which influence each other. Teddlie and Tashakkori (2009) identify that analyses can proceed in parallel, and crossover of research types may be feature. For example, it may be profitable to quantify qualitative data ('how often did someone make a comment or statement'), and to qualify quantitative data (e.g. produce a description of different subsets within the quantitative data analysis).

With mixed methods analyses, the final analysis integrates and brings the inferences and explanations together in a **meta-inference**. The mechanics of this process are not always made clear. One way of keeping track of findings as they arise, which is applicable here, is to write theoretical memoranda as findings and themes emerge (Miles and Huberman, 1994). In practical terms this can be as simple as writing sticky notes of main findings and arranging them on a whiteboard to look for similarities and differences as the data are analysed. Although this is a very simple technique, it is surprisingly powerful and can help make sense of otherwise very confusing sets of data.

Both triangulation and mixed methods allow research to be developed using a range of investigations. The next two sections illustrate frameworks for including these in a research project which is both rational and cohesive.

Hallmarks of quality in quantitative research

A hallmark is a mark or symbol which guarantees quality. This section will identify research hallmarks, so that the reader can make reasonable decisions about the quality of published research. Traditionally, the quality of research has been discussed under two main headings: Validity and Reliability. These have been applied to both qualitative and quantitative research. They are not necessarily easy qualities to understand, and indeed within the research communities ideas occasionally change when considering applicability of these to different types of research. To introduce this topic, here is an example which might help illustrate these concepts. For this example to work, the reader needs to know that, at the time of writing, in Leicester nurse education takes place at the Charles Frears Campus of De Montfort University (DMU). There are a number of charming villages on the outskirts of Leicester which have nothing to do with De Montfort University: Scraptoft and Coalville are two of them.

Is the bus service valid and reliable?

Every morning the number 10 bus arrives outside my house at 08:30 and takes me to the Charles Frears Campus of DMU.
It is both reliable and valid.

It arrives on time, but sometimes takes me to Coalville.
It may be reliable but is not valid.

Sometimes it arrives one hour early, but still goes to the campus.
It may be valid, but is not reliable.

Sometimes it arrives at midday and takes me to Scraptoft.
It is neither valid nor reliable!

Translating from this example, **validity** can be seen to be an assessment of how well the research addressed the original research question, i.e. *'Did it take you where you wanted to go?'*, or in more research-orientated terms, *'Did you answer the question which you set out to answer?'*.

Reliability, in contrast, assesses the repeatability or stability of the research. Was the research reliable? *Could it be used time after time to produce accurate results?*

Validity and reliability depend upon each other, which can make discussion of their individual components confusing. For this book it has been decided to discuss validity first, because this is probably where most small-scale researchers are likely to start, by trying to put together a research tool which explores the issues identified in their research question or hypothesis. Once the validity has been addressed, and to some degree assured, it may then be reasonable to start using it in pilot samples, at which point its reliability could realistically be explored. As a final note to this introduction, issues of validity and reliability are seldom resolved. A piece of research is never shown to be either 100% valid or 100% reliable; rather, in a well-conducted piece of research these issues are addressed and evidence that they are present is given. Therefore the final judgement of whether validity and reliability have been met is not on the paper, it is in the judgement of the reader.

How to support validity in quantitative research

In Chapter 2, when discussing survey literature, a case was made for providing the provenance of questionnaire items; this, it was suggested, supported the validity of the research. It is now time to explore this quality further. In general, it is quite difficult to pin down exactly what validity is, particularly when discussing it in the context of quantitative research. This is because it cannot be directly measured by quantitative or statistical methods (unlike reliability). Instead, it is necessary to review and discuss the research undertaken and look for both its strengths and weaknesses.

Most standard research textbooks supply a glossary of terms. Here is how two popular examples define validity. Polit and Beck (2008, p. 768) define validity as '*the degree to which an instrument measures what it is intended to measure*': in terms of the earlier example, this is a bus which really *does* take you to the university! This corresponds positively with most other writers; for example, DeVon *et al.* (2007, p. 155) define validity as the '*ability of the instrument to measure the attributes of the construct under study*'. In more everyday language, this equates to 'Did you measure what you set out to measure?', and logically 'Did you answer your research question?'. Thus studies with low validity may well be in-depth and may answer a number of questions – but not necessarily the ones they set out to answer!

Reading about validity also shows that there are a number of components within it. Unfortunately, as Bannigan and Watson (2009) point out, there are rather too many; currently at least 35 different items have been put forward. For the purpose of this writing, Polit and Beck's (2008) categories will be used, partly because this book is widely in use in the UK, comes from a highly reputable source, is aimed at researchers working in healthcare, and should be readily available for consultation by students, but mostly because the three main headings are conceptually clear.

A lot of discussion of validity is based around research tools, specifically scales to explore psychometric instruments, for example measures of mood, attitudes and adaptation to illness (DeVon *et al.*, 2007). To discuss it within the context of this book, we will use an example with this in mind. Norrie and Dalby (2007) used a survey to investigate how student nurses learned, and in particular whether their learning style could be characterised as being 'adult' in nature (andragogic) or 'child' like (pedagogic). A questionnaire was produced and administered to students in years one, two and three of their nursing programmes. This was based upon the work of Malcolm Knowles, an influential educationalist (Knowles, 1998). The following passages will explore whether this study contains evidence of the different types of validity.

I Internal validity

Internal validity is described most easily in terms of an experiment. The question which the researcher should ask is 'has the effect which I have discovered come from the independent variable (in experimental terms), or has it been caused by another confounding variable – that is a variable which has not been recognised and interferes with the results (Polit and Beck, 2008). This is always possible – one candidate might be a Hawthorne effect (discussed in Chapter 5), caused by the subjects being part of a research study itself (Bowling, 2009). A well-conducted experiment will be set up to control this happening by careful sample selection and by randomisation into treatment groups. Surveys are perhaps more susceptible, as no effort is (usually) made to provide a control. Applied to Norrie and Dalby's (2007) research, internal validity is an issue. For example, as the students move from year one through to year three, do they become more exhausted and disillusioned? Are these confounding factors which the research does not take into consideration? Hindsight is always perfect, and in retrospect it might have been better to include other questions to explore (for example) how anxious, or fatigued the students felt, to try to find other factors which might, or might not explain the results.

2 Construct validity

As Polit and Beck (2008, p. 299) point out '*research cannot be undertaken without using constructs*'. A construct is an abstract idea or concept. DeVon *et al.* (2007) state that each item within a research instrument (for example a survey questionnaire) should address an aspect of the construct which is being investigated. In practical terms this means that when constructing the questionnaire, care must be made to show that the items included are relevant to the research question, and ideally that they address a specific aspect of it. An extreme example of bad practice would be the researcher who sits down at his or her desk and draws up a questionnaire using only their own knowledge and experience. It is quite possible that the items in the questionnaire are relevant, but there is no proof, and it seems likely that personal bias will compromise the validity of the questionnaire.

By contrast, Norrie and Dalby (2007) based their research on the model (or construct) which they wished to explore. Critical parts of Knowles' work were copied and circulated. Three focus groups were conducted, where sample statements were developed for inclusion in the questionnaire to explore the main elements within Knowles' theory. Therefore a sustained effort was made to support construct validity by a direct link between the theory and the survey. Another way to support construct validity is to use or amend an existing research tool. There are a number of questionnaires already in existence, such as the Hospital Anxiety and Depression Scale (Zigmond and Snaith, 1983), which as the name suggests explores issues of anxiety and depression and has been used in clients within the hospital and outpatient setting, and the various Short Form questionnaires (e.g. SF-36, SF-12), which are commercially available and have been shown over a long period of time to be valid (and reliable too) (SF-36.Org, 2010).

3 External validity

External validity is a measure of how well the findings relate to the real world. Bowling (2009) relates this to sampling: if the sample is well chosen, then the results can reasonably be expected to be relevant to that defined group of people. For example, if conducting research into the effect of tri-cyclic antidepressants such as Amitriptyline on chronic pain, the researchers would think carefully about who to include within their study. Ideally the group would be self identifying, that is people with chronic pain. However, chronic pain is a large and diverse group in itself. Does the research question really identify such a broad group – or might it be more specific; people with neuropathic pain (pain caused by damage to nerves, for which there is a *prima facie* case for effectiveness), or people who have (for example) arthritis, which is both painful and chronic, but is unlikely to respond to these therapies. Again, the correct research question or hypothesis emerges as the critical factor in initiating high-quality research. Another factor is sample size. Small studies are at risk of compromising external validity as small studies involve the risk of sampling bias, and type 2 error. This where an effect exists, but the sample size is too small to demonstrate it. This also raises the issue of how large the sample is, which is discussed in Chapter 5.

In terms of Norrie and Dalby's (2007) paper, the study was interested in how student nurses developed their learning over the three-year period of their nursing studies. Therefore a sample was chosen from years one, two and three to follow this progression. A sample size of 321 was used – this was the total number of students who could be persuaded to complete the questionnaire. However, the return rate was only 57%, so bias in response may be present, which could limit the external validity of the work.

Reliability

Bowling (2009, p. 468) defines reliability as '*the extent to which the measure is consistent and minimises random error (its repeatability)*'. Similarly Polit and Beck (2008, p. 730) define it as '*the degree of consistency or dependability with which an instrument measures the attribute it is designed to measure*'. Bannigan and Watson (2009) use the example of a pole which is claimed to measure one metre in length to illustrate the concept. No matter who approaches the pole, it remains the same length. It is therefore completely reliable. This also addresses Bowling's (2009) second criterion: there can be no random error in the pole itself. In research terms this means that if the research were repeated it would provide (roughly) the same results, no matter who undertook it. For example, if we undertook a survey of how much readers of this book understood the world of research on the Monday (on a scale from 0 to 10), and then repeated it on the Tuesday, assuming that they had not read the whole book in between (or possibly even if they had!) the results would be expected to be similar, if not exactly the same. If this was the case, then the survey could be described as reliable. Note that the second use of the survey is very unlikely to produce identical findings. There is always going to be random variability in the research, but this is acceptable and can be measured and its effect quantified. The beauty of quantitative research is that we can measure reliability in research designs. Here are some ways to do this:

- **Test–retest reliability**: A process for exploring this has been described above. For ordinal and interval data, a coefficient of correlation will be produced. As discussed in the quantitative data section, a coefficient of 1 would indicate identical data sets, which in reality is unlikely to happen. A coefficient of greater than 0.8 would be considered to be high and would suggest satisfactory reliability (Field, 2009). This criterion is also termed *stability* by some authors. Although attractive (it is at least an easy to understand concept), it has a drawback. It is expensive in terms of resources, since it means essentially doing the survey twice, so researchers should think twice before including it in a design. One option might be to do a test–retest reliability analysis on two smaller pilot groups, for example.
- **Inter-rater reliability**: This is very useful where participants are being observed. If a researcher observes someone and records data, they are described as being 'raters'. For example, hand hygiene is currently (and probably always will be) a big issue in healthcare. If a survey is taken of how long people wash their hands, then inter-rater reliability could be addressed by two researchers simultaneously observing the same group of participants washing their hands. The findings would then be analysed, again using a coefficient of correlation. At this point, you may think, '*but*

if observers are watching the same event, then surely they must *record the same data!'*. This is not always the case, however. In the example given it would depend (amongst other things) on how well the research has been designed. For example, exactly when does the hand washing start? Is it:

–   When the participants turn on the tap?
–   When the water touches the hands?
–   When soap is applied?
–   When hand washing movements are first observed?
–   Some other index left up to the choice of the observer?

Therefore to support reliability, a well formulated research protocol with clear definitions of the included variables is essential.

■   **Internal reliability**: Are the data homogeneous? Homogeneous is a research term which serves to confuse, rather than clarify. It simply means, 'of the same kind', indicating that the data are all showing a similar picture, or are 'pointing in the same direction'. Here is an example. If I invite a group of students to my house for dinner, and use a questionnaire to explore a number of factors which contribute to the quality of the evening, on a scale from 0 to 10, I might include the following elements:

1.   The quality of the starter
2.   The selection of wines on offer
3.   The quality of the main course
4.   The quality of the dessert
5.   The choice of cheeses
6.   The conversation and company
7.   The background music

If half of the diners really enjoyed every aspect of the evening, they would give high scores for all of these. The responses would be homogeneous. Similarly, if the other half of the diners really hated every aspect of the evening, then the responses would also be homogenous. Taken together as a group, the findings would still be internally homogenous, because although their responses fell into two distinct groups, the responses within *each questionnaire* would still all be 'pointing in the same direction'. If, however, there was a mix, for example groups of people who gave high scores to items 1, 3, 6 and 7, but clearly did not enjoy 2, 4 and 5, then the results are not homogeneous; they are instead heterogeneous, meaning there are different groups within the data. In (very) laypersons' terms the data are 'lumpy'. This can be assessed by a number of techniques, one of which is **alpha analysis** The most common version of this is Cronbach's alpha, but others are available. This measures the relationship between each item in the questionnaire with every other item. It is expressed in the same way as correlations, e.g. a figure of 1.00 shows a set of data which are completely internally valid. In most situations, a figure of 0.7, or ideally 0.8 and above, shows that the data have reasonable internal reliability (Field, 2009). This is important, because it means that if the data are internally consistent they can be summated. This means that they can safely be added together and an average generated. This is very helpful for anyone who uses a bank of Likert statements or similar type of scale. If we use the example above , if the Cronbach alpha value is high, for example greater than 0.7, then to give an overall summary of how well the meal went, I can take the average sum-mated score for each person who attended and generate the mean, median and mode; if the data are parametrically distributed then a standard devia-tion becomes valid. This is a sound way to bring together a large amount of data and produce clear overall findings; it would provide a single effective measure of how well the dinner went.

Bringing validity and reliability together

These characteristics do not exist in a vacuum. There is also nothing magical about them. If the research starts off with a clear and precise research question, then to some extent both validity and reliability will be built in. The researcher then needs to think carefully at each step of design, sampling and analysis, referring the process back to the research question. Giving an appropriate rationale for each step of the process tends to support both. Finally, *research-ers must always pilot their work.* Please note the emphasis. This means using a small-scale trial of the research before devoting time and resources to a full-scale piece of work. Vital feedback from this can then be built into the defini-tive investigation; not to do so threatens both validity and reliability.

Research and evidence: what are the links and differences?

Throughout this book there has been an emphasis on the application of research findings to influence and underpin clinical practice. Research is a major source of evidence, but there is more to evidence-based practice than finding a promising piece of research and then changing one's own practice. Any positive changes thus produced will be piecemeal and may, quite reasonably, attract opposition. What are the skills necessary to develop evidence-based nursing practice? A good place to start is to consider the types of evidence which are available.

In the 1990s Guyatt, working with Sackett and others (Guyatt *et al.*, 1995), produced a very influential hierarchy of evidence, aimed primarily at medical staff. Research was divided into five classes, from Class I, the most robust, through to Class V, the least robust. This hierarchy is still in use, notably in the UK by the National Institute for Clinical Excellence, amongst others and is summarised in Figure 8.2.

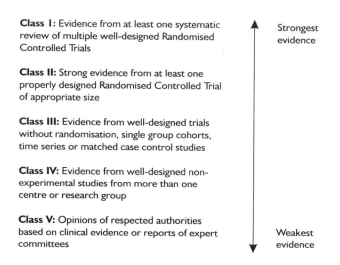

Figure 8.2 Hierarchy of evidence.

This hierarchy (and others) remains influential, but it does have some limitations and implications for nursing that require exploring.

Class I is the strongest and is composed of systematic reviews of a number of Randomised Controlled Trials (RCTs). A systematic review uses explicit and rigorous methods to critically appraise and bring together findings from a number of studies (Mulrow and Cook, 1998). They should be transparent, repeatable and comprehensive and report their methods, so in fact they closely resemble the research process itself. The aim in a systematic review is to compare a range of studies, extract information, bring the findings together and produce robust findings in a meta-analysis. If it is accepted that RCTs are a particularly robust form of evidence, then it is clear that a review composed of RCTs will, in effect, result in a set of findings from an RCT which is larger than the contributing studies- you may remember that in the world of quantitative research bigger really is better!

Systematic reviews are a large topic in themselves, and will not be explored further in this book. There is some good information on how to construct systematic reviews available from the Centre For Reviews and Dissemination (CRD) at York University, UK (http://www.york.ac.uk/inst/crd/funding.htm). Of possibly greater interest is the Cochrane Library (see exercise below).

Class II should be familiar for readers of this book: it contains a single or a few RCTs. Similarly, Class III includes a mix, but these can be described as quasi-experimental studies; studies with some, but not all, of the qualities of a true experiment. They commonly lack randomisation between groups of participants. This impairs their ability to identify cause and effect. Class IV moves out of the realm of experiment altogether, and could include surveys, case studies or even action research projects. Finally, Class V contains a mix of other slightly vague categories; you get the feeling that the authors had rather lost interest here. What is particularly interesting for nurses is that qualitative research is not included in the hierarchy at all. This is not unusual given that it was developed for medical staff who function largely within the scientific tradition.

Cochrane Library

The Library is named after Dr Archie Cochrane, an early pioneer in evidence-based practice. Of particular interest within the library is the Cochrane Database of Systematic Reviews. This is available from http://www.thecochranelibrary.com/.

Within the UK it currently appears to be available free of charge for two page summaries, but in the USA there are reports of limited availability due to charges being imposed. If you have trouble accessing it, use an academic library website from a local university for example, or from a NHS Trust.

Cochrane Library exercise

Log on to the Cochrane website (URL above). Take a look through the 'Highlighted New and Updated Cochrane Reviews' section on the first page. Scroll through three of the reviews and get a feel for the type of evidence used, the methods and the way that information is provided. Take some time to reflect on whether this format would be helpful to you in developing your practice.

Accessing evidence

One of the problems with trying to access evidence is that there is so much of it! This is an issue which Archie Cochrane identified and was one of the drivers in setting up the Cochrane Library. Approximately 20,000 trials are published each year and around 1,000 articles are added each day! Fortunately we also live in an age where we can use technology to address this and simplify our choices, through the use of databases. Before discussing finding evidence through a database, it is worthwhile to introduce some terms.

- **Sensitivity (recall)**
  This is a measure of the comprehensiveness of a search method, i.e. its ability to identify all relevant articles on a given topic. Highly sensitive strategies tend to have low levels of precision and vice versa.

  In other words, the search may result in large numbers of articles, but not all will be relevant.

- **Specificity (precision)**
  This is a measure of your search strategy's ability to produce articles which deal effectively with your topic, and describes the ability of a search to exclude irrelevant articles. A high-specificity search may result in too few articles, but of these a high number are likely to be relevant.

There are two main types of searches:

- **Unfiltered databases**
  Examples of these include the British Nursing Index (BNI) and the Cumulative Index of Nursing and Allied Health Literature (CINAHL). These are accessible through most UK university libraries. If unsure, ask your local librarian. As the name suggests, the BNI is produced by a group of British Libraries, and CINAHL operates out of California. Taken together, the majority of the English language publications relating to nursing can be accessed by these through a computer keyboard.

  Using suitable key words, a very quick search can easily be undertaken. To help this process, every year more articles can be accessed as full text. The key words can be referred to as *inclusion* terms; articles which have these terms in their titles or attached key word tabs will be picked up by the search engine. The sensitivity of the search is an issue: amongst the large number of articles, some and possibly most of them, may not be relevant. Boolean operators such as 'AND' are helpful here, as they direct the database to identify articles which include a number of key words. A good tip is to include the term 'AND nurs*'. AND is the Boolean operator, and the use of the truncation symbol (*) means that any term which includes the four letters 'nurs' will be picked up, e.g. nurse, nurses, nursing etc. The word on its own is of little use (there are over 300,000 articles currently tagged with it in the BNI), but when it is incorporated with another search term (e.g. 'Down's Syndrome'), it increases specificity markedly, so that only articles which have a significant nursing content are found. Otherwise the researcher has to wade through highly technical articles on chromosome structure! Even so, the use of inclusion criteria only may result in too many articles. Commonly, therefore, it is necessary to start *excluding* some articles, and this could be done according to:

- **Date**: for example to exclude articles older than five or 10 years
- **Language**: typically to only include articles written in English
- **Full text**: if there are really large numbers, then it is possible to be fussy: the searcher can specify only references which include full text, excluding all others.

■ **Filtered databases**

In a filtered database, a number of filters are already in place. The example used here is provided by PubMed, a medical database which is produced by the US National Library of Medicine. As above, it is easy to access through the Internet, and is freely available globally. It can be used similarly to the BNI and CINAHL as an unfiltered database, but in the home page of PubMed is the heading 'PubMed Tools'. Within this there is a link 'Clinical Queries'. This section has a set of filters built in to it, so that any key words which are entered automatically have an extensive set of filters applied to provide results based largely upon randomised clinical trials – very much working within a medical, scientific paradigm.

Using information to make clinical decisions

According to Glasziou *et al.* (2003), the first step in using good quality information is to set an answerable question. One way to do this is to set a PICO. The letters identify P for Population (or Patient), I for Intervention, C for Comparator or Control and O for Outcome.

PICO Example I

Here is an example: my daughter has a dog bite on her leg. It looks clean and does not require stitches. Should I take her to our General Practitioner for prophylactic antibiotics? Using the PICO format I produce a question:

Should someone who has a dog bite (P) take antibiotics (I) rather than just observe the wound (C) for infection (O)?

In key words this is summarised as:

P   dog bite
I   antibiotics

C   observation

O   infection

Putting these terms into PubMed clinical queries produces a number of results. At the time of writing (May 2010), there is one direct hit of a small scale study showing no difference between wounds treated with prophylactic antibiotics and those without; but this is quite old, has a limited sample size and uses an antibiotic not currently used in the UK (Elenbaas *et al.*, 1982). Stronger evidence is available on the same page with a direct link to a systematic review from the Cochrane Library entitled 'Antibiotic prophylaxis for mammalian bites' (Medeiros and Saconato, 2001).

As discussed earlier, Cochrane Library reviews are as good as it gets in the world of evidence-based medicine, and sit at the top of the quantitative hierarchy of evidence, so within five minutes it is possible to put together a PICO, enter it into a database and, with a little interpretation, get strong evidence for guidance.

What does the evidence show?

Medeiros and Saconato's (2001) review showed that the use of prophylactic antibiotics was associated with a statistically significant reduction in the rate of infection after bites by humans. However, prophylactic antibiotics did not appear to reduce the rate of infection after bites by cats or dogs. Prophylactic antibiotics were associated with a statistically significant reduction in the rate of infection in hand bites.

Given that my daughter was bitten by a dog in her leg, there is no evidence to suggest that prophylactic antibiotics will be helpful, and assuming her tetanus is up to date I decide to adopt a policy of 'watch and wait'.

Exercise: DIY PICO!

Take five minutes to produce a PICO of your own. This could be about something which has concerned you in practice, but for a change think about your family and friends. Does your uncle Bill, for example have a cough which won't go away? Does your sister complain of headaches, are you worried that all this research has made you drink too much alcohol?

Put your PICO in the British Nursing index, (BNI), or a similar database.

Take 10 minutes to look at the results. Decide whether you have been:

Too specific: this is essentially where your search has been too fussy and by including all the terms which you wished it has 'overshot', resulting in very few, and possibly no, hits.

The remedy here is to remove some keywords – are all these terms really necessary? Start to remove some of the less important ones and see if the number of hits increases.

Too sensitive: this is where your search is too broad – you have lots of hits, but it would take too long to look through them. The remedy here is to start to include some more key words. Think about how you can narrow your focus. As you add terms, see what it does to the number of hits: they should decrease.

Personal preference will differ, but one way to judge how good you are with your search strategy is to identify how many hits you would be willing or able to sift through on screen over a period of 10 minutes. As a start, aim for a total number of hits no greater than 15.

PICO Example 2

Here is another example of using PICO, with a little more mathematics involved. I am going to travel to a conference on research methods in Singapore. I have a friend who suffered a Deep Vein Thrombosis (DVT) from a similar long-haul flight, and I am wondering if I should purchase some support stockings for the flight. My PICO therefore is:

P   Air travel
I   Stockings
O   Deep Vein Thrombosis

NB: a comparison was not included, as the comparison was with travellers who did not wear stockings. The greater the number of terms included, the greater the specificity, but the lower the sensitivity. This may be a matter of personal preference, but on the whole it is preferable to have a broader set of sources and then select the study which best meets the clinical query.

As with Example 1, a Cochrane systematic review was found (Clarke *et al.*, 2006), entitled 'Compression for preventing deep-vein thrombosis in airline passengers). This reviewed 10 randomised trials which compared groups of travellers who wore compression stockings with those who did not. The total number of participants was 2,856.

In these trials 50 travellers on long-haul flights out of a total of 2637 were found to have DVT. Three had worn stockings, 47 had not.

Some mathematics; which group was more at risk?

The risk to a flyer who does not wear compression stockings therefore is 47 divided by 2637, which equals = 0.0178 (or 1.78%)

The risk to a flyer who does wear compression stockings therefore is 3 divided by 2637= 0.0011 (or 0.11%). There is clearly a reduction between the two groups, but by how much?

Relative risk = risk of outcome in the stocking group, divided by the risk of outcome in the non-stocking group= 0.0011/0.0178 = 0.062

This tells us how many times more likely it is that an event will occur in the treatment group relative to the control group. A relative risk less than 1 means that the treatment reduced the risk of the outcome. If RR were greater than 1, then we would conclude that the treatment had *increased* the risk of the outcome taking place. Clearly a risk reduction has taken place, showing that wearing compression stockings has had an impact on the occurrence of DVTs.

What else do the mathematics tell us?

If we want to get a measure of whether it is helpful to wear compression stockings in real life situations, it may be best to work out the Absolute Risk Reduction (ARR), and the Number Needed to Treat (NNT).

As the name suggests, ARR tells us about the absolute difference between the two groups. It is found by subtracting the two rates.

ARR = risk of DVT in the non-stocking wearing group minus the risk of DVT in the stocking wearing group. For this example:

ARR= 0.0178 – 0.0011 = 0.0167

This tells us that wearing compression stockings decreases the chance of DVT for someone undergoing a long distance flight by 1.67%.

The differences between the two groups therefore are relatively small. At this point it might be worth thinking about whether this small change in risk is worth pursuing. Compression stockings, after all, are really not fashionable!

The final way to address this is to look at the Number Needed to Treat (NNT).

NNT is useful, it tells us how many people would need to wear stockings in order to prevent one case of DVT. This is worked out by dividing the ARR into 1 (1/ARR). In mathematical terms it is the reciprocal of the ARR.

For this example, $1/ARR = 1/0.0167 = 59.8$

This tells us the number of people we need to apply stockings to in order to prevent one case of DVT, i.e. we need to apply stockings to 60 people to be confident that we have reduced the incidence of DVT by one in a population. The Number Needed to Treat tells us not only whether a treatment works but how well it works. It is useful to healthcare professionals because it gives information on the effort needed to achieve a particular outcome (Talluri, 2005).

What you may have decided by now is that the numbers have limitations. There is a beneficial effect due to wearing compression stockings, but it is small. If you are in a low-risk group, then you may decide that it is not really worth the cost of buying or the rigmarole of applying compression stockings. However, the review is not only about statistics. In the report, some expert opinion is also applied. Clarke *et al.* (2006) also point out that wearing stockings had a significant impact in reducing oedema of the lower legs and that no significant adverse effects of wearing stockings were reported. Therefore if you are in a risk group for DVT, or from previous experience found that flying gave you uncomfortable swollen legs, you may decide that it is worth the cost and trouble to wear stockings.

A mathematical exercise

Essential thrombocythaemia is a condition in which the bone marrow produces too many platelets. Amongst other things, this puts people at risk of clotting and potentially experiencing strokes and heart attacks. An RCT was conducted by Harrison *et al.* (2005) of two medication regimes. One was for hydroxyurea, an established drug which has some rather unpleasant side effects, but definitely reduces platelet counts. The other drug was anagrelide, which had fewer serious side effects and theoretically might be a preferred option. In a total sample size of 809, the participants were randomised into two groups and treated with the drugs as follows. The total number of blood clots per group was recorded. For this example, we will treat the hydroxyurea group as the control, and compare it with the 'new' drug anagrelide. The data are summarised below:

Drug	Number in group	Number of clots
Hydroxyurea plus aspirin	404	36
Anagrelide plus aspirin	405	55

Work out the risk for each group

Risk for hydroxyurea group =

Risk for anagrelide group =

What is the **Relative risk** for a patient taking anagrelide compared to hydroxyurea? Is this greater than or less than one? What does this tell you?

Relative risk = <u>**Risk for anagrelide group**</u>
                         Risk for hydroxyurea group

(answers given at the end of the chapter)

Number needed to harm

The relative risk shows that the new drug (anagrelide) is actually more harmful than the older control (hydroxyurea). The effect is the opposite of the previous example; instead of now calculating the Number Needed to Treat, we now calculate the Number Needed to Harm (NNH). Otherwise the process is identical:

What is the **Absolute Risk**?

Absolute risk = 0.1356 − 0.0891 = 0.0465

What is the number needed to harm?
NNH is found by dividing the ARR into 1 (1/ARR).

Therefore **NNH** = 1/0.0465 = 21.50

This means for every 22 patients who take anagrelide, there will be one who experiences a blood clot, in comparison with the hydroxyurea group.

NB: this was taken to be so strong an effect that the trial was completed early and the recommendation was made that hydroxyurea should be the main treatment for this condition.

Relating evidence to nursing

The PICO is nothing if not focused. Indeed, Glasziou and his group intended it as part of the armoury of the busy General Medical Practitioner in the UK who is faced with a rapid presentation of patients at surgery and who has approximately two minutes to put a query together and find an answer to it.

The PICO, specifically when it is linked to filtered databases such as PubMed Clinical Enquiry, is perhaps *too* focused. It can be likened to a lighthouse, which sends out a beam of extremely bright light, but surrounding this is a vast shadow. It trades a very high specificity for a low sensitivity. In general, in nursing at least, it can be suggested that broader, more sensitive, searches may work better, reflecting the fact that there are some major differences between the ways that medical and nursing staff look at and use evidence. For medical staff, evidence is primarily quantitative in nature and closely linked to large RCTs. It is used to explore the effectiveness of therapies. This is an important goal, but the evidence really only addresses one type of question: 'Does therapy A work better than therapy B?'.

For nurses this is too limiting. One significant difference is in the use of qualitative research, which as the earlier chapters of this book has shown, is a major tool for nurses who wish to develop their practice. Sackett (who coined the phrase 'evidence-based medicine') *et al.* (2001, p. 1) suggested that the best research evidence should be *'clinically relevant research, often from patient centred clinical research'*. The topics chosen for medicine are commonly focused on diagnostic tests and treatments, and may be addressed properly using the Evidence Hierarchy. Nursing is broader and must therefore use a broader range of evidence. Topics chosen for practice development are often situated within the interpretivist paradigm, therefore evidence for these should also be sought within the interpretivist paradigm (Smith *et al.*, 2004): for example 'What are our clients' experiences?' or 'How can we support our patients further?'. This means that both qualitative and quantitative research should be used to provide evidence-based nursing practice. Within the discussion regarding case studies and participatory action research, the researcher had freedom to chose which research methods best answered the research questions; similarly, when developing a nursing evidence base, we have to ask what are the areas of practice we wish to develop and within which paradigm do they exist, and following this we must identify where we would look for the best evidence.

Final exercise: construct your own hierarchy of evidence

In reading this book, you will have learnt about many different ways to do research, and to identify evidence. This final exercise is one that only you can do. On a separate piece of paper, mind map all the different types of research and evidence that you have read about.

Now give them a score, starting with the strongest. Identify the types of research which you would be essentially confident to base your own practice upon, most of the time. You could do this by giving a percentage score to each, where:

- 100% would be types of research or evidence that you would always feel confident in using to make practice decisions
- 50% where you might be confident (roughly) half the time in using to make practice decisions
- 10% would be evidence that you would perhaps not use on its own, but might have some value in a larger context

As you can see, it is not possible to be too categorical about attaching these scores, so do it quickly, without too much internal debate.

Use these weightings to construct your own hierarchy as in Figure 8.2, above.

Finally, compare the two. You may now be able to make decisions about your own evidence outlook. Are you largely an interpretivist, with a leaning towards qualitative data sources, or are you a positivist, more confident in scientific enquiry? Are you somewhere in between? Are you just confused? One possible solution is the use of a pragmatist paradigm, as suggested by Teddlie and Tashakkori (2009), when discussing mixed methods research. To be pragmatic means to focus on practical rather than theoretical considerations and it could be argued that this is congruent with nursing generally, nurses being based in practice rather than theory. The logical extension of this perspective would be to commend mixed methods to nurse researchers, where the research question dictates the methods rather than belonging to a 'qualitative' or 'quantitative' camp.

Whichever you choose, you have clarified something important for your future practice.

Answers for hydroxyurea/anagrelide exercise

Risk for hydroxyurea group = 36/404 = 0.0891 (8.9%)

Risk for anagrelide group = 55/405 = 0.1356 (13.56%)

Relative risk = 0.1356/0.0891 = 1.5219. This value is greater than one, meaning that the people in the anagrelide group were more likely to have a blood clot than those in the hydroxyurea group.

References

Anthony, D. (1999) *Understanding Advanced Statistics*. Churchill Livingstone, London.

Anthony, D. (1996) A review of statistical methods in the *Journal of Advanced Nursing*. *Journal of Advanced Nursing*, **24**(5), 1089–94.

Argyrous, G. (2005) *Statistics for Research With a Guide to SPSS*, 2nd edn. Sage, Thousand Oaks, CA.

Ashing-Giwa *et al.* (2002) Understanding the breast cancer experience of women: a qualitative study of African American, Asian American, Latina and Caucasian cancer survivors. *Psycho-oncology*, **13**(6), 408–28.

Bannigan, K. and Watson, R. (2009) Reliability and validity in a nutshell. *Journal of Clinical Nursing*, **18**, 3237–43.

Benner, P. (1984) From novice to expert: excellence and power in clinical nursing practice. *The American Journal of Nursing*, **84**(12), 1480.

Bowling, A. (2009) *Research Methods in Health: Investigating Health and Health Services*, 3rd edn. Open University Press, Buckingham.

Bowling, A. and Ibrahim, S. (2005) *Handbook of Health Research Methods*. Open University Press, Maidenhead.

Bryar, R. (1999) An examination of case study research. *Nurse Researcher*, **7**(2), 61–78.

Bryman, A. (2001) *Social Research Methods*. Oxford University Press, Oxford.

Campbell, K. (2006) *Myeloproliferative Disorders*. Leukaemia Research, London.

Capewell, S., Morrison, C. E. and McMurray, J. J. V. (1999) Effects of the Heartbeat Wales programme. *British Medical Journal*, **318**, 1072.

Carr, W. and Kemmis, S. (1986) *Becoming Critical. Education, Knowledge and Action Research*. Falmer, Lewes.

Clarke, M., Hopewell, S., Juszczak, E., Eisinga, A. and Kjeldstrøm, M. (2006) Compression stockings for preventing deep vein thrombosis in airline passengers. *Cochrane Database of Systematic Reviews*, Issue 2. Art. No.: CD004002. DOI: 10.1002/14651858.CD004002.pub2.

Cleave, C. (2009) *The Other Hand*. Sceptre, London.

Cott, N. F. (1987) *The Grounding of Modern Feminism*. Yale University Press, New Haven.

Denscombe, M. (2007) *The Good Research Guide: for Small-scale Social Research Projects*, 3rd edn. Open University Press, Maidenhead.

Denzin, N. and Lincoln, Y. (2000) *Handbook of Qualitative Research*, 2nd edn. Sage, Thousand Oaks, CA.

Department of Health (2000) *The NHS Plan*. Crown Copyright. London.

DeVon, H., Block, M., Moyle Wright, P., Ernst, D., Hayden, S., Lazarra, D., Savoy, S. and Kostas Polston, E. (2007) A psychometric toolbox for testing validity and reliability. *Journal of Nursing Scholarship*, **39**(2), 155–64.

Dick, B. (2005) *Grounded Theory: A Thumbnail Sketch*. Resource papers in action research. http://www.scu.edu.au/schools/gcm/ar/arp/grounded/.

Dyson, S. and Brown, B. (2006). *Social Theory and Applied Health Research*. Open University Press, Berkshire.

Dyson, S., Culley, L., Norrie, P. and Genders, N. (2008) An exploration of the experiences of South Asian students on pre-registration nursing. *Journal of Research in Nursing*, **13**(2), 163–76.

Dyson, S. E. (2005) Global boarders: Leaving Zimbabwe – factors influencing undergraduate student's decision to study nursing in the UK. In: *Health Economics Management and Policy* (eds. J. N. Yfantopoulos and G. T. Papanikos), pp. 135–72. Athens Institute for Education and Research, Athens.

Elenbaas, R., McNabney, W. and Robinson, W. (1982) Evaluation of prophylactic oxacillin in dog bite wounds. *Annals of Emergency Medicine*, **11**(5), 248–51.

Field, A. (2009) *Discovering Statistics Using SPSS*, 3rd edn. Sage, Thousand Oaks, CA.

Fink, A. (1995) *How to Ask Survey Questions*. Sage, Thousand Oaks, CA.

Finlay, L. (2008) A dance between the reduction and reflexivity: explicating the 'phenomenological psychological attitude'. *Journal of Phenomenological Psychology*, **39**, 1–32.

Fowler, J. and Norrie, P. (2009) Development of an attrition risk prediction. *British Journal of Nursing*, **18**(19), 1194–200.

Geertz, C. (1973) *The Interpretation of Cultures: Selected Essays*. Basic Books, New York.

Gillham, B. (2000a) *Developing a Questionnaire*. Continuum, New York.

Gillham, B. (2000b) *Case Study Research Methods*. Continuum, London.

Glaser, B. (1978) *Theoretical Sensitivity: Advances in the Methodology of Grounded Theory*. Sociology Press, California.

Glaser, B. G. and Strauss, A. L. (1967) *The Discovery of Grounded Theory: Strategies for Qualitative Research*. Aldine, Chicago.

Glasziou, P., Del Mar, C. and Salisbury, J. (2003) *Evidence Based Medicine Workbook*. BMJ Books, London.

Grbich, C. (2004) *New Approaches in Social Research*. Sage, London.

Greasley, P. (2008) *Quantitative Data Analysis Using SPSS: an Introduction for Health and Social Science*. Open University Press, New York.

Grey, M. (2009) *Evidence Based Healthcare and Public Health*, 3rd edn. Churchill Livingstone, Edinburgh.

Guyatt, G. H., Sackett, D. L., Sinclair, J. C., Hayward, R., Cook, D. J. and Cook, R. J. (1995) Users' guides to the medical literature; a method for grading health care recommendations. *Journal of the American Medical Association*, **274**, 1800–4.

Hammersley, M. (1990) *Classroom Ethnography: Empirical and Methodological Essays*. Open University Press, Milton Keynes.

Harrison, C. N., Campbell, P. J., Buck, G., Wheatley, K., East, C. L., Bareford, D., Wilkins, B. S., van der Walt, J. D., Reilly, J. T., Grigg, A. P., Revell, P., Woodcock,

B. E. and Green, A. R. (2005) Hydroxyurea compared with anagrelide in high-risk essential thrombocythaemia. *New England Journal of Medicine*, **353**(1), 33–45.

Holloway, I. (1997) *Basic Concepts for Qualitative Research*. Blackwell Science, Oxford.

Holloway, I. and Walker, J. (2000) *Getting a PhD in Health and Social Care*. Blackwell Science, Oxford.

Husserl, E. (1970) *Logical Investigations* (transl. D. Carr). Humanities Press, New York.

Key, J. (1997) *Research Design in Occupational Education: Qualitative Research* (Module 14). Available at http://www.okstate.edu/ag/agedcm4h/academic/aged5980a/5980/newpage21.htm; accessed 25 April 2010.

Kitto, S. *et al.* (2008) Quality in qualitative research. *Medical Journal of Australia*, **188**(4), 243–6.

Knowles, M. S. (1998) *The Adult Learner: a Neglected Species*, 5th edn. Gulf, Houston.

Lester, S. (1999) *An Introduction to Phenomenological Research*. Stan Lester Developments, Taunton.

Lewins, A., Taylor, C. and Gibbs, G. R. (2005) *What is Qualitative Data Analysis (QDA)?* Available at: http://onlineqda.hud.ac.uk/Intro_QDA/what_is_qda.php; Accessed 25 April 2010.

McNiff, J. and Whitehead, J. (2006) *All You Need to Know About Action Research*. Sage, Thousand Oaks, CA.

Medeiros, I. M. and Saconato, H. (2001) Antibiotic prophylaxis for mammalian bites. *Cochrane Database of Systematic Reviews*, Issue 2. Art. No.: CD001738. DOI: 10.1002/14651858.CD001738.

Merleau-Ponty, M. (1962) *Phenomenology of Perception* (transl. C. Smith). Routledge & Kegan Paul, London. (Original work published 1945.)

Miles, B. and Huberman, M. (1994) *Qualitative Data Analysis: An Expanded Sourcebook*, 2nd edn. Sage, Thousand Oaks, CA.

Morgan, D. L. (1997) *Focus Groups as Qualitative Research*. Sage, London.

Morton-Cooper, A. (2000) *Action Research in Health Care*. Blackwell Science, Oxford.

Mulrow, C. C. (1998) *Systematic Reviews: Synthesis of Best Evidence for Health Care Decisions*. American College of Physicians, Philadelphia.

Munro, B. H. (2005) *Statistical Methods for Health Care Research*. 5th edn. Lippincott Williams & Wilkins, London.

Murray, S. and Graham, L. (2009) Practice-based health needs assessment: use of four methods in a small neighbourhood. *British Medical Journal*, **308**, 1443–8.

Norrie, P. (1997) Time utilisation of nurses in intensive care. *Nursing in Critical Care*, **2**(3), 121–5.

Norrie, P. (2004) Expanding the case study, the narrative thread. *NT Research*, **9**(1), 30–7.

Norrie, P. and Dalby, D. (2007) How adult are our students? A cross sectional exploration of the learning characteristics of nursing students in a United Kingdom university. *Journal of Research in Nursing*, **12**(4), 319–29.

Norrie, P. and Anthony, D. (2004) Are clinical information systems acceptable to critical care nurses? Some findings and a reliable and valid tool for further research peer reviewed research paper. *Information Technology in Nursing*, **16**(1), 12–18.

Norrie, P. (2003) What do critical care nurses want from clinical information systems? *Information Technology in Nursing*, **15**(4), 10–15.

NRES (2008) National Research Ethics Service (NRES) Homepage. Available from http://www.nres.npsa.nhs.uk/ (accessed 3 October 2009).

O'Cathain, A., Murphy, E. and Nicholl, J. (2008) The quality of mixed methods studies in health services research. *Journal of Health Services Research & Policy*, **13**(2), 92–8.

Oppenheim, A. N. (1992) *Questionnaire Design, Interviewing and Attitude Measurement*. Pinter, London.

Parahoo, K. (2006) *Nursing Research, Principles, Processes and Issues*, 2nd edn. Palgrave Macmillan, Basingstoke.

Phillips, E. and Pugh, D. (2005) *How to get a PhD: a Handbook for Students and Their Supervisors*, 4th edn. Open University Press Buckingham.

Polit, D. F. and Beck, C. T. (2008) *Nursing Research: Generating and Assessing Evidence for Nursing Practice*, 8th edn. Lippincott, Williams & Wilkins, London.

Polkinghorne, D. (1988) *Narrative Knowing and the Human Sciences*. University of New York Press, New York.

Pope, C. and Mays, N. (2000) *Qualitative Research in Health Care*, 2nd edn. BMJ Books, London.

Riessman, C. (1993) *Narrative Analysis*. Qualitative Research Methods Volume 30. Sage, London.

Rolfe, G. (2006) Validity, trustworthiness and rigour: quality and the idea of qualitative research. *Journal of Advanced Nursing*, **53**(3), 304–10.

Rosenbaum, M. (2006) Was drug trial payment too high? Available from http://www.bbc.co.uk/blogs/opensecrets/2006/11/tgn1412.html (accessed 23 December 2009).

Sapsford, R. (2007) *Survey Research*, 2nd edn. Sage, London.

Sarantakos, S. (2005) *Social Research*, 3rd edn. Palgrave MacMillan, Basingstoke.

Seidal, J. V. (1998) *Qualitative Data Analysis*. Available from http://www.scribd.com/doc/7129360/Seidel-1998-Qualitative-Data-Analysis/ (accessed 25 April 2010).

SF-36.Org (2010) *The SF Community*. Available from http://www.sf-36.org/ (accessed 26/02/10).

Shields, L. and Twycross, A. (2008) Sampling in quantitative research. *Paediatric Nursing*, **20**(5), 37.

Sim, J. and Sharp, K. (1998) A critical appraisal of the role of triangulation in nursing research. *International Journal of Nursing Studies*, **35**(1), 23–31.

Smith, P., James, T., Lorentzon, M. and Pope, R. (2004) *Shaping the Facts: Evidence Based Nursing and Health Care*. Elsevier, Edinburgh.

Talluri, S. K. (2005) Number needed to treat (or harm). *World Journal of Surgery*, **29**(5), 576–81.

Teddlie, C. and Tashakkori, A. (2009) *Foundations of Mixed Methods Research: Integrating Quantitative and Qualitative Approaches in the Social and Behavioural Sciences*. Sage, Thousand Oaks, CA.

Thomas, M., McKinley, R., Mellor, S., Watkin, G., Holloway, E., Scullion, J., Shaw, D., Wardlaw, A., Price, D. and Pavord, I. (2009) Breathing exercises for asthma: a randomised controlled trial. *Thorax*, **64**, 55–61.

Wadsworth, Y. (1998) *What is Action Research?* Action Research International. Available from http://www.scu.edu.au/schools/gcm/ar/ari/p-ywadsworth98.html (accessed 25 April 2004 2010).

Yin, R. (2009) *Case Study Research: Design and Methods*, 4th edn. Sage, Thousand Oaks, CA.

Zigmond, A. and Snaith, R. (1983) The Hospital Anxiety and Depression Scale. *Acta Psychiatrica Scandinavica*, **67**, 361–70.

Index